£7.99

Study Skills

CW01072772

Written by Merryn Hutchings and Helen Schmitz

Published by Scholastic Ltd,
Villiers House,
Clarendon Avenue,
Leamington Spa,
Warwickshire CV32 5PR

© 1996 Scholastic Ltd
Text © Merryn Hutchings and Helen Schmitz

Authors Merryn Hutchings and Helen Schmitz
Editors Deborah Martin and Clare Gallaher
Assistant Editor Jean Coppendale
Designer Claire Belcher
Illustrations by Maggie Downer
Cover design by Lynda Murray
Cover photograph by Martyn Chillmaid
Designed using Aldus Pagemaker
Printed in Great Britain by Clays Ltd, Suffolk

British Library Cataloguing-in-Publication Data
A catalogue record for this book is available from the
British Library.

ISBN 0-590-53164-6

Contents

Introduction

WHY STUDY SKILLS?

The development of study skills is an important area of children's education, involving finding, organising, evaluating and presenting all kinds of information. These skills are necessary if children are to become independent learners.

When children start school they have already developed a range of learning skills. Young children gather information from a variety of sources. They observe, play, listen and ask questions. They gain information from their families and friends, from nurseries and playgroups, from television and from participating in everyday life. One of the roles of the school is to develop and refine these existing skills, and to offer children opportunities to access and use a wider range of information skills, such as reading and using maps, graphs, tables and computers.

Today we live in a society which is dominated by information. Many jobs involve accessing, organising and transmitting information, or providing technology for handling information. With such a large store of available information it is possible to teach children in schools only a very small fraction of what they may need to know in their lifetimes. It is crucial, therefore, that they gain skills in locating, interpreting and using information. Study skills will continue to be developed throughout the educational process, but the foundations are laid in the primary years.

A major aspect of study skills is accessing and collecting information. Children need to develop their strategies for observing and asking questions. They need to learn how to locate relevant information in books and to develop different reading strategies appropriate to the task in hand. In addition, they should learn how to use maps, atlases and globes and to acquire the specific skills needed for the interpretation of graphs, tables

5

and diagrams. It is also vital that children learn to make effective and confident use of information technology.

But study skills are not simply about gaining access to information and collecting it. Children also need to develop skills which will help them to assess and evaluate the information they have. They need to be able to identify their own purposes clearly and to assess whether the information they find is relevant to those purposes. They also need to be able to distinguish general ideas from detail. They will need to compare and contrast information obtained from different sources, and to be aware of the possibility of bias and of potential sources of inaccuracy. This will involve distinguishing fact from opinion.

Children also need to learn to present the outcomes of their investigations. They need to be aware of their audience and to take it into account when selecting information and making decisions about appropriate forms of presentation. These could include written accounts, displays and performances. Children will increasingly become aware of different writing styles and of a range of ways of presenting information: graphs, diagrams, tables, photographs, cartoons and so on.

STUDY SKILLS AND THE CURRICULUM
Study skills are not specific to any single curriculum area: rather, they permeate all areas of the curriculum. Nor are study skills specific to any age range: they should be developed throughout the primary years.

Speaking and listening, reading and writing all form part of the curriculum in English. The use of information books and reference materials should be encouraged from the early years.

The science curriculum involves a range of investigational skills including experimenting, observing and measuring, and using primary and secondary sources. Children are expected to evaluate the information they gain and to use a wide range of methods, such as diagrams, graphs and tables, to present their findings. Handling data also features in the mathematics curriculum.

Information technology is specifically concerned with the use of IT equipment and software to store and retrieve information. It also involves the communication of ideas and information in a variety of forms appropriate to the needs of the audience.

Both history and geography specify that children should learn to ask and answer questions, and to select, analyse and record information relevant to the topic. In history children learn to use a range of sources of

historical information, such as documents, artefacts, pictures and buildings. Geography involves the development of specific skills in the use of globes, maps and plans at a variety of scales.

Generally, study skills are more effectively developed in a meaningful context: that is, children will see more point in learning *how* to access information when they actually need to do so. Exercises to develop specific skills are less effective when they have no other purpose. Thus the majority of the activities in this book are set in the context of wider classroom activities or projects. However, a few activities take the form of games which can be carried out in odd moments.

THE STRUCTURE OF THIS BOOK

The book is divided into eight sections. Five of these focus on different kinds of information: books and the printed word, oral sources, information from maps, media sources, numerical data.

The next two sections are rather different. Technology for information brings together a range of ideas involving the use of technology for accessing, handling and presenting information. The section on bias and evidence focuses on the need to assess and evaluate information obtained from any source. The aim is to help children distinguish fact from opinion and consider possibilities of bias and inaccuracy.

The final section sets out two examples of projects with a strong focus on study skills. Each of these shows how, in the context of a project, children can develop skills in accessing, evaluating and using information from a variety of sources.

Books and the printed word

The activities in this section involve finding and using information in books. Children need to be able to access such information. This involves making use of library catalogues, and the contents page, index and headings in information books, as well as dictionaries, glossaries and thesauri. Effective use of these sources involves knowledge of the alphabet and skills of locating items in alphabetical lists quickly and efficiently.

It is important for children to understand that information books are designed to be dipped into. They do not need to start reading at the beginning and work through to the end: indeed this would be a most inefficient way to use many books. Children should develop reading strategies for using reference books effectively: skimming to gain an overall impression, scanning to locate information, and detailed reading to obtain specific information.

It is important too that children learn how to make use of the information they find in books. Criticism has been levelled at work in primary schools where children have copied passages straight out of the books without necessarily understanding what they are writing. The instruction to 'put it in your own words' is not particularly helpful: this is a difficult thing to do. Some of the activities in this section are designed to help children set their own questions and use reference books for their own purposes, which may be different from those of the author.

Our pets

Age range
Five to seven.

Group size
Whole class or smaller group.

What you need
Paper, pencils, crayons, felt-tipped pens, book-making facilities (spiral binder or book press).

What to do
Explain to the children that they are going to make their own information books about pets. Discuss with them what sort of books they could make. One possibility would be to make a big book to which each child contributes a page about their pet, real or imaginary. This book could also include block graphs showing how many pets are owned by children in the class, what colours they are, their ages and so on.

Another idea would be to make a book of instructions for looking after the classroom pets. This could include advice on feeding, cleaning and playing with the animals. The book would be designed for practical use and could be made to look professional by using photographs as illustrations.

Children often prefer to read books they have made themselves. These books are about things which are familiar to them and the language used is the children's own language. Such books can be placed in the classroom book corner. You can then encourage children to look at other books on the same topic and help them to choose information books they will enjoy.

Follow-up

Some children might like to make their own books, individually or in small groups, focusing on the needs and care of particular types of pet.

Alphabet fun

Age range

Five to seven.

Group size

Whole class.

What you need

Paper, pencils, felt-tipped pens, colouring pencils.

What to do

The aim of this activity is to introduce the alphabet to very young children when they first come into school and to continue to reinforce alphabet skills for the older children. Learning the alphabet is an integral part of understanding how our language system works. So much of our information is categorised in alphabetical form that children need to gain knowledge and understanding of how the alphabet works from an early age.

Learning by association can prove to be fun. Talk about the initial letters of the children's names, and then think of an adjective to describe them. The adjective must use the same initial letter as the child's name, for example Happy Hannah or Jumping Jonathan.

Ask the children to draw a picture to go with the name. You could write the captions for the children under their drawings. If the initial letter is highlighted in another colour, when the drawings are displayed around the classroom (in alphabetical order of course!) the alphabet will stand out clearly.

Not all children will be able to think of an adjective that begins with the initial letter of their own name, so you will need to challenge the more competent children in the class to think of adjectives to go with the more difficult or less used letters, for example Zany Zac.

Follow-up

Go through the names regularly with the children, starting from the beginning of the alphabet. Ask them questions like, 'Who comes before Happy Hannah?' or 'Who comes after Jumping Jonathan?' Invite them to ask each other questions: 'Is it true that Grinning Gavin comes before Singing Sadia?'

Alphabet frieze

Age range

Five to seven.

Group size

Small groups of two to five children.

What you need

A camera, possibly some props such as outdoor PE equipment, bats and balls (be creative), paper and pens, plenty of space.

What to do

In a large space, ask the children, working in groups, to explore making letters with their bodies. They could make the shape of the letter by lying on the floor, or they could use large apparatus or wall bars to balance upon. Encourage the children to use their imagination to explore letter shapes. If they find some letters difficult, let them use pens and paper to try out ways of creating the letters.

When you are satisfied that the children have completed the alphabet in one way or another, take individual photographs of each letter. Mount the 26 letters as a frieze for children to refer to.

Follow-up

Children could draw illuminated letters of the alphabet, and these could also be displayed. There are many beautiful books on calligraphy which offer examples of styles of lettering and illumination, for example *Creative Calligraphy* by Peter Halliday (Kingfisher, 1992), *Pen Lettering* by Ann Camp (A & C Black, 1984) and *Writing and Illuminating and Lettering* by Edward Johnston (A & C Black, 1994).

Other ideas might be to make the letters completely out of small stars, or to use small letters of the alphabet to make one large letter, or even to use punctuation marks. The possibilities are endless. Each time, however, refer the children to the order of the alphabet, which will help them with their dictionary skills.

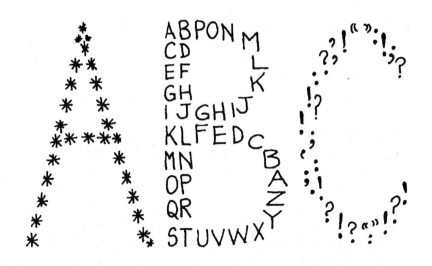

Animal alphabet book

Age range
Five to seven.

Group size
Whole class working individually.

What you need
Paper, pencils, coloured pencils, glue, scissors or a cutter, an art easel with large sheets of paper clipped to it. You will also need to make a large book with at least 26 pages.

What to do
The purpose of this activity is to provide a resource which can be stored in the class book corner. The book will help children to learn to read books that are organised alphabetically. It will also help to develop their vocabulary, their knowledge of names of animals, and their use of the English language.

As a whole class, talk about names of animals and suggest an adjective to describe each animal. Remind the children that both words must share the same initial letter: for example, angry aardvark, prickly porcupine or wiggly worm. As the children make suggestions, write them down on a large sheet of paper so that everyone can see them.

Next give each child the name of an animal to draw, reminding them to draw the animal as 'angry', 'prickly', 'wiggly' or whatever adjective is used. When they have finished, ask them to write the caption under the picture in clear lettering and then to go over their pencil writing with black felt-tipped pen to make the lettering stand out. Let the children stick their pictures in the appropriate order in the book. You might need to give some assistance here, depending on the maturity of the class.

If there are more children in your class than letters in the alphabet, there is always the front cover to be designed, along with the contents page, the back cover, and perhaps details about the 'authors' of the book! When it is completed, cover the book in self-adhesive plastic film to make it more durable and place it in the book corner.

Follow-up
Make some small books for the children to create their own individual alphabet reference system. In pairs, brainstorm as many words as possible, beginning with a letter from the alphabet, for example 'J' – Jeremy, Jack, James. Ask the

children to group words into similar categories, for example names, food, animals, and suggest that they write a simple poem. For instance,
Jeremy, Jack, James
They are all names.

January, July, June,
It will be my birthday soon.

Jam, jelly...

The poems can be put into little books called 'alphabet poetry books'.

Alphabet sandwiches

Age range
Five to eleven.

Group size
Whole class or smaller group.

What you need
A poster showing the alphabet. You may also need a dictionary.

What to do
This game is designed to help children put words in alphabetical order. It can be played when the children are sitting on the carpet.

Ask one of the children to suggest a word – any word will do. For example, if 'paint' is suggested each child should try to think of one word which will come before it in alphabetical order and one word which will come after it.

Someone might suggest 'apple' and 'train'. Ask if anyone can suggest two words which will be closer to 'paint' in alphabetical order. Examples might be 'orange' and 'queen'. It is possible to get still closer, using, say, 'pail' and 'pat'.

With younger children, focus on alphabetical order by first letter, and refer to the alphabet poster. Older children should be able to use second and even third letters, as in the example above.

When no one can get any closer to the word, the children could look in the dictionary and see which words are listed immediately before and after their word.

Follow-up
Let the children investigate the words printed at the top of each page in the dictionary. Can they work out which two words sandwich the words on any particular page?

The categorising game

Age range
Seven to eleven.

Group size
Whole class, working individually or in small groups, no more than four.

What you need
Paper, pencils.

What to do
This activity will help to improve the children's skills for placing items into categories. Select a category from the following list, and write it on the board. Ask the children to brainstorm as many items as they can which belong to the group that the category describes:

- something you eat;
- something made of plastic;
- something made of wood;
- an animal;
- a vegetable;
- an item of clothing;
- a fruit;
- a flower;
- a famous building;
- a city.

Once you have exhausted this list, invite the children to offer any more ideas of their own. They may notice that some of the above categories can be subdivided to make further categories, such as 'something you eat – a savoury food or a sweet food', 'a city – a city in Britain or a city

Column 1	Column 2	Column 3
something you eat	t	tomato

abroad'. (The subdivisions can be chosen according to the ages of the children you are working with.)

Give the children photocopiable page 111. In the first column there are various categories listed. Ask the children to choose a letter of the alphabet and write it in the second column for each category. In the third column, the children must then try to write down as many entries as possible for the category in column one, starting with the chosen letter in column two.

Follow-up
When they have completed their sheets, ask the children to write a story using all the entries suggested for one category.

Spelling advice

Age range
Five to eleven.

Group size
Whole class working in groups.

What you need

A space on the display board, A4 paper, felt-tipped pens.

What to do

This is an ongoing activity in which the children offer their fellow pupils advice about spellings of difficult words, spelling rules, easy ways to remember spellings and so on.

Set aside an area of display space to make a spelling advice board. You will need space for about ten A4 notices of spelling advice. Each group in turn might be responsible for the board for a week. In the group, individual children will make the notices.

An advice notice should include the difficult word, written in large letters in felt-tipped pen, and should also indicate the spelling rule which will enable other children to remember it. For example:

there means a place and is spelled like **here**

Some notices might draw attention to spelling rules or to groups of words which have a common pattern. As the teacher, you might also want to contribute a word each week, perhaps something related to the class topic. The notices on the board could be arranged in alphabetical order, like a dictionary.

When the class is gathered together, get the children who have made the notices to talk about this week's words. Encourage children to refer to the board and use the words in their writing.

Follow-up

In their individual wordbooks, encourage children to write notes about how to remember the way each word is spelled, rather than simply listing correct spellings.

Topic glossary

Age range
Five to eleven.

Group size
Whole class.

What you need
Examples of information books with simple glossaries, space on a display board, A4 paper, felt-tipped pens.

What to do
Explain to the children that a glossary is a bit like a dictionary. It contains an alphabetical list of new or unusual words relating to a specific topic and explains their meanings, and is usually shorter than a dictionary. Show them the examples you have collected.

Explain that every topic studied will include some new or unusual words, or words used in a specialised way. When children come across unfamiliar words in their topic work, they should look them up in a dictionary. (In some reference books they will find a glossary which will explain the words used.)

Ask the children to write each new word in large letters on a piece of paper and to write an explanation of what it means in relation to this topic. They may want to include examples of the way the word is used, copying out the relevant sentence from the reference book.

Some words are more easily explained by illustrations. For example, the words 'poop' and 'prow' could be explained by a picture of a ship with appropriate labels. For younger children picture glossaries are the most useful.

All the sheets should be pinned up on the display board, to form a class glossary. Encourage children to check the glossary whenever they come across a new word, and to add to it. Draw attention to the topic glossary by talking at the end of each day about new words which have been added.

When all work on the topic has been completed, the sheets can be arranged in alphabetical order to make a topic glossary book.

Follow-up

Children may like to make glossaries for their individual folders of topic work.

Setting the questions

Age range

Five to eleven.

Group size

Whole class working individually or in pairs.

What you need

Paper, pencils, photocopiable page 112 (optional).

What to do

This activity involves children setting and investigating their own questions about a class topic. It is a useful one to do when the class has just embarked on a new topic. As usual, you will need to introduce the topic to them, perhaps through a visit or a film which will arouse their interest. The next session can be spent identifying what they already know and what questions they would like to answer during the next few weeks.

Older children can compile written lists of questions about the topic. Talking with a partner will help them to think of questions which interest them. Younger children can work as a group to identify questions, with the teacher acting as scribe. Photocopiable page 112, the KWL chart, can be used to record children's responses.

When all the children have made lists, you could collect them and group the questions under headings. Talk about the list of questions with the whole class. How can each question be answered? Are there any questions on the list which may prove impossible to answer? Could they be turned into questions which can be answered? (For example: 'How many dinosaurs were there?' may be impossible to answer, whereas 'How many species of dinosaur were there?' will prove more feasible.)

Discuss with the class how they want to set about answering the questions. One approach would be for each child to research their own questions. However, this may lead to a lot of repeated work, as some questions will probably be raised by more than one child. An alternative would be for the class to work in groups, each group tackling a specific area of linked questions. They would need to display their findings so that all the other groups could read them.

The advantage of this approach to topic work is that children will look at information books with very specific questions in mind. They are more likely to use the books for their own purposes and less likely to copy passages verbatim.

Sharing information books

Age range
Five to eleven.

Group size
Whole class or smaller group.

What you need
Information books that children are currently using in topic work.

What to do
This is an activity to do when the children are sitting on the carpet. You might want to use the time at the end of the day, when you would normally read a story. The idea is to have a time for sharing information books and reading them aloud. Children are used to enjoying stories together, but less often have opportunities to share their factual discoveries and enthusiasms.

Ask the children to bring the information books they have been using for their topic work that day. What did they read which they found interesting, surprising or puzzling? Encourage the children to talk to the group about the books they have been reading and the things they have found out. You will probably know of some children who have made interesting discoveries during the day and you can encourage these children to contribute.

This activity can be adapted for different age groups. Younger children who are not fluent readers may have found interesting pictures in their books which they want to show and talk about. You could contribute to this sharing by reading aloud from some of their information books.

Older children and more fluent readers should be encouraged to read short passages from their information books to the group. (As you circulate during project sessions you could ask particular children if they would be willing to read certain passages to the group. They will then be able to prepare by looking through the passage.)

You can also encourage children to share passages which they find particularly difficult to understand. This may be more appropriate with a smaller group rather than with the whole class.

These sessions could also be used to discuss how the children located the information which interested them. Did they skim through the book, looking at headings and illustrations? Did they use the contents page or the index? One difficulty children will sometimes encounter is that the word listed in the index may not be the one they expected. For example, 'wheat' may be indexed as 'cereals', or 'washing' as 'laundry'. It is worth spending some time discussing alternative words to look up. A thesaurus may be helpful here.

This difficulty may also be encountered when children need to consult subject indexes in the library. Invite the children to talk about any difficulties they may have had in accessing information, and get the class to suggest strategies which may help.

Follow-up

Talk with the whole class about how information books are written. How do the authors find out the information? Would they have used primary sources (for example, historical documents) or simply have made use of other information books? How can the reader judge the accuracy of the information presented? Examine the books to see what is said about the authors' expertise or qualifications. Look also at the date of publication and discuss what types of information books might quickly become out of date.

Making a class dictionary

Age range
Five to seven.

Group size
Whole class.

What you need
Felt-tipped pens, an easel. You will also need to make a large book with 26 pages, graduated at the side like an address book.

What to do

Young children need access to as much written language as possible. Even if you operate an emergent approach to writing in your class, children still need plenty of contact with correctly written forms of the English language. This activity will provide a basic dictionary of correctly spelled words.

Place the book on the easel where everyone can see it. Ask the children, taking turns, to tell you the letters of the alphabet in order, while you write them down at the edge of the appropriate page. Then talk with the children about important words that you may need for your topic or theme. Decide together where each word should go, then write it on the appropriate page. At this stage it will be too difficult to group the words within each page in alphabetical order, so just list them according to the initial letter, as they are suggested.

Once the children start writing, they can use this dictionary as a form of reference. Encourage them to use it to check their spellings.

Follow-up

Individual children may like to have their own wordbooks for their own special words. Make them smaller books in the same style for easy reference and get them to label the pages alphabetically themselves. They may be able to transfer words from the class book themselves, or you can fill in the words for them. It is important that they build up a knowledge of words, or strategies to find the words they need, so that they can begin to work independently. Encourage the children to ask each other for help, too.

Human dictionary

Age range
Seven to eleven.

Group size
Small group.

What you need
Paper, pens.

What to do

This short physical activity practises dictionary skills, in particular alphabetical order using more than the initial letter and the use of headwords on a dictionary page.

Choose two words that will serve as headwords for a dictionary page. Write each one on a separate piece of paper and give one each to two children. Then, depending on the number of children in the group, write other words that might appear on that dictionary page on separate pieces of paper, one for each remaining child. Tell the 'headword' children to stand at the front of the room, one at each end, displaying their word. Give the remaining

building
barn
brick
bungalow
balcony

castle
church
chimney
cottage
chapel

children a word each and tell them to organise themselves between the two headwords in alphabetical order. Discuss any problems of order that occur. To increase the difficulty, introduce a time element, either setting a time limit or timing their effort and getting them to try to improve on that the next time the game is played.

Class word bank

Age range
Five to seven.

Group size
Whole class, but used by individuals.

What you need
Two pieces of material 1m × 1m, small pieces of card to fit into the pockets, needle, thread, scissors.

What to do
Word banks are very important resources in the classroom as they can play a useful part in encouraging children's word retrieval skills.

First, sew 26 pockets on to the material and label them in alphabetical order. Into these pockets you will place the word cards. You might need two loops at the top of the material so that you can hang it on a piece of dowelling or hooks. When you have made your word holder, make sure that the pieces of card are not so small that they can be easily lost. They should be large enough for young hands to manipulate them. The writing on the cards should be clearly readable. The word bank should consist of words that are regularly used. It should also include words that the children request. Let the children take turns to tidy the word bank to

make sure the cards are in alphabetical order. This constantly reinforces their alphabetical knowledge and their understanding of the language system.

You will need to check through regularly and remove words that are no longer required. On occasions you may like to add picture clues to help very young children. Always encourage the children to help each other when retrieving particular words.

Follow-up
Children can be encouraged to use a word bank as an additional source of information gathering. They can use it as a class dictionary so that they have an extra place to look for words in support of their independent writing.

What does it mean?

Age range
Seven to eleven.

Group size
Groups of four.

What you need
Paper, pens, pencils, card, age-related dictionaries, thesauri.

What to do
Cut some thin card into 10cm × 10cm squares. Choose a number of words from the dictionary, selecting appropriate words for the age and ability of the children in your class. Write each word on two separate cards in large letters. On one card write down the real meaning of the word; on the other card write an incorrect meaning.

Give each group a selection of cards. Taking one word at a time, ask two children in the group to read the word and the definition to the other two members of the group. The two listeners have to say which definition is correct. They then take it in turns to look in the dictionary for the correct definition. Make sure that the children take turns to read the cards and encourage them to work together to help each other.

When they have gone through all the cards, ask the children to quiz each other by offering the meanings of the word. The others have to say what the word is and spell it correctly.

Follow-up
Make another set of cards. This should contain words that have similar meanings and one word that has a dissimilar

meaning. The children have to find the 'odd one out'. They can use a thesaurus to help them. Reinforce their learning by having quiz sessions either in small groups or within the whole class.

Dictionary races

Age range
Seven to eleven.

Group size
Whole class or smaller group.

What you need
Each child will need a dictionary. (They do not necessarily have to be identical dictionaries.) It will be helpful to have an alphabet on display.

What to do

The aim of dictionary races is to help children develop strategies to enable them to flick quickly through the dictionary to find the right place and then to scan the page to locate a particular word without having to read every word on the page. It is best to use this activity in short but frequent sessions in which new skills are developed step by step.

The game involves asking the children to find a particular word as quickly as possible. When they have found it they should put one hand up and point to the word in the dictionary with the other hand.

In order to locate words efficiently and quickly children will need to acquire several skills. First, they need to be able to estimate where in the dictionary they will find words beginning with a particular letter of the alphabet. Encourage them to do this by asking how far through the dictionary they expect to find words beginning with, say, 'm'. (The alphabet on display will help them to estimate accurately.) Then challenge them to open the dictionary at what they estimate is the right place. They should open the dictionary cleanly and not turn any pages over. How many children have words beginning with 'm' on their pages? How far out were they? Children will need plenty of practice at this before they move on to the next stage.

Once they can find the initial letter they are looking for quickly (and without searching through from the beginning of the dictionary), move on to activities involving the second letter of words. There are two skills involved here. First they need to be able to make a reasonable guess at what the second letter might be from the sound of the word. Some letter combinations are obvious but others are less so (for example, 'my' at the beginning of 'mystery'). Children also need to understand the way in which words are listed alphabetically. Having identified the 'm' section, they need to know whereabouts in it they might find a word beginning with 'mi', for example. They can use a similar estimating technique to that described above.

Follow-up

Children working in pairs could set each other similar tasks, using an encyclopaedia.

Quiz time

Age range

Seven to eleven.

Group size

Whole class working individually.

What you need

A small display board, a collection of information books relating to the class topic, small pieces of card.

What to do

The aim of this activity is to encourage children to search for specific information in reference books, rather than simply using whatever information the book gives them. It also encourages them to keep a note of the sources of the material they use. The activity will take up a small part of the children's time in their regular topic work sessions over a period of about two weeks.

As children investigate the class topic using information books, ask them to note particular facts with a view to setting a quiz question for other children to answer. Each child sets one question relating to the topic. The answer to the question must be available in one or more of the information books. Ask the children to write their questions on small cards and display them on the notice-board. The child who sets the question should keep a note of the answer and of the book and page number where the information was found. When the cards are all displayed you will need to code them with either numbers or letters for reference.

Allow the children some time during topic sessions to look up answers to the questions other children have set. They can attempt as many or as few questions as they want to. It is likely that they will be able to answer some very quickly because they will have read the same reference book; others may present a greater challenge. They will probably need help to use the books effectively. They will need to look at the contents page and the index and to be able to scan the text to find the relevant material. Encyclopaedias could also be included. In this case children will need to learn that the topics are usually organised in alphabetical order.

Ask the children to write down their answers to the questions, together with the title of the book and the number of the page where they found the information. They should keep their answers in their topic folder. At this stage answers

should not be shared because children will tackle the questions in a different order.

At the end of a specified time (one or two weeks) spend a period as a whole class going through questions and answers and comparing the sources used. This sort of quiz is more valuable than one which simply tests knowledge but does not offer children any opportunity to research for themselves.

What's my number?

Age range
Five to seven.

Group size
Whole class in groups of four.

What you need

Paper, pencils, a telephone directory as an example. It will be helpful to have an alphabet on display.

What to do

The ability to use an indexing system is an important life skill. Giving young children experience of working with such systems will increase their ability to locate information quickly and efficiently.

Talk about the importance of knowing telephone numbers in case of an emergency. Ask the children, in small groups, to write down their surnames, their addresses and their telephone numbers (being aware of any sensitive situations within the class). Then ask each group to list the names and numbers, as in the telephone directory, in alphabetical order of surname. Children will need to learn how to list names where there is more than one with the same initial letter. Refer them to the alphabet on display.

Two children from each group should then swap groups in order to add more names to the list. Keep going until all the names in the class have been added to the list. Either rewrite or type the lists into a class directory.

Follow-up

Use index cards as another way of storing information alphabetically. You could add other useful numbers like the local health centre or library, or numbers the children think are important.

Making information books

Age range

Nine to eleven.

Group size

Whole class working in pairs.

What you need

Access to information books in class, school and public library, book-making facilities (spiral binder or book press), a class of infant children to work with.

What to do

Tell your class that they are going to make some information books for the infant class. Each pair of children can be teamed with a pair of infant children.

The first step will be for the junior children to interview the infants to find out what sort of information books they like. Help the children to plan this interview in advance. What will they need to ask the infants? They might want to talk with them about the design of books and look at books which the infants enjoy. Do they prefer mainly illustrations

Once text and illustrations are complete, the book can be put together. It will need to be sturdy, with card covers protected by plastic. It is not much fun having a book which falls to pieces! Finally the books can be taken to the infant class and presented to the children they were designed for. Maybe the juniors could read the books with the younger children.

This activity has considerable benefits for infants as well as juniors. The infants will need to look at a range of information books in order to decide what they want. They will also enjoy the books that are made. Having a book made to your own specification gives a considerable feeling of importance. The juniors, meanwhile, will have to consider the needs of the audience they are writing for. Their research in information books will have a specific purpose.

with captions, or cartoons, or pop-up books? The juniors will also need to ask the younger children what sort of information they would like in their books. The general topic may be decided by the infants' class topic, but they could ask the infants exactly what they would like to know about the topic.

After the interview the juniors will need to research the topic, locating appropriate information for the infants and making notes. Once they have all the necessary information, they can then write the text and design the book. They will need to find ways of presenting the information which the younger children will be able to understand. This might involve simplifying the vocabulary or using illustrations to help explain the text. (It will be helpful to have a range of books for younger children in the classroom so that they can see how other authors have solved these problems.)

What's the difference?

Age range
Five to eleven.

Group size
Whole class working in pairs.

What you need
A collection of photographs from different decades (for example, the 1990s, the 1970s and the 1940s) showing similar items, postcards from galleries or museums that show differences in time or cultures.

What to do
Give each pair of children a set of pictures and ask them to try to identify similarities and differences. For example, they

could look at hairstyles, types of clothes, shapes of cars and so on. They might focus on the concept of 'change' when comparing photographs of different decades. What is the difference between clothes, or buildings, or transport, in the 1990s and the 1940s, for example?

Younger children could bring in photographs of their parents and grandparents, and spend time discussing like and unlike, again perhaps focusing on clothes and hairstyles. Older children could make historical comparisons using postcard evidence. An example might be to compare the Moghul dynasty in India with the Elizabethan era in Britain. What important issues arise? For example, how much do the children know about Indian history?

Follow-up
Young children could use a large sheet of paper to make a simple chart showing like and unlike. Older children could write some careful comparisons based on the evidence from their discussions.

Journey 1850

Age range
Nine to eleven.

Group size
Whole class or smaller group (depending on availability of information books).

What you need
A range of reference materials about Victorian times and the history of transport, encyclopaedias, atlases or maps of Great Britain, writing materials.

What to do
This activity will be spread over several sessions. Tell the children that they are each going to write and illustrate a first-person account of a journey – not a journey they have done themselves, but they must imagine that it is 1850. You could specify the starting point and destination (say, London to Edinburgh) or allow the children to choose. They can make up fictional incidents (accidents, robberies and so on that happened on the journey) but they must get all the historical facts correct.

Before the children begin to write, the whole group could discuss what they will need to find out in order to write their stories. For instance, they will need to know how people travelled in 1850. It would be possible to make this journey using various forms of transport, such as coach, train or boat. Each child will need to decide on a form of transport and find out what the vehicle would look like. How long would the journey take? What would the cost of the journey be? Would they stop at night? If so, where? What would they be wearing? What food could they buy to eat on the journey? How could they communicate with the relatives or friends awaiting them at their destination?

Having identified the main questions, they will need to research the topic and make brief notes. These should indicate which book contains specific information, what page it can be found on, and the relevant facts. Encourage the children to share their information and advise each other on the best sources. Which aspects of the topic do they find hardest to locate? Are there any other sources that might help (for example, a local history or society, or a museum)? Researching and writing the story will continue in parallel; the children will come across new questions to investigate as a result of writing.

Writing historical fiction is a useful activity for several reasons. The child feels a sense of ownership over her work. There is usually little temptation to copy straight from reference books because the child's purpose is different from that of the books. Children are able to direct the story to make use of a wide variety of information which they may find interesting.

It is also a challenging task. It is all too easy to slip out of the historical context by using a phrase such as, '...and then I switched the light off and went to sleep'! Children enjoy trying to make every detail of their story correct.

Oral sources

It is important – and required – that children should develop skills in speaking and listening. Most children enjoy talking but are not always enthusiastic about listening to others. Ideas and strategies to help them learn to take turns in speaking and to respect the speaker's right to be heard need to be creative and relevant.

In infant classes children should learn to take part in discussions, relating their contributions to what has already been said and asking and answering appropriate questions. Older children should be able to pick out the main points of an argument and to evaluate what they hear, using questions to probe and clarify ideas. Skills of organising talk are also important, if talk is to be an effective tool for learning. Children can be helped to recognise the main points of an argument and to structure talk, for example in a discussion or an interview.

The activities in this section are designed to help children to reflect on their own oral skills and to develop them.

News time

Age range
Five to seven.

Group size
Whole class.

What you need
No special requirements.

What to do
Use news time as an opportunity to encourage the children to develop their skills in listening and asking questions.

The children sit on the carpet in a circle and one child at a time tells the rest of the class her news. Encourage the other children to ask questions which will help to clarify and expand the news item they have heard. At first you will probably have to ask some questions yourself, to provide a model for the children.

You could also contribute your own news item, but deliberately keep back some vital information so that the children have to ask questions. For example:

'I went out with my daughter.'
'Where did you go?'
'I went into town.'
'Did you go shopping?'
'No, I didn't.'
...and so on.

As the children gain more confidence you could discuss which questions are most helpful in extracting more information.

Encourage the children to indicate when they have something to ask, and not to call out. In a discussion waving hands can be very distracting, so try to develop less obtrusive systems. When children are sitting in a circle a raised finger is quite visible.

Voicing opinions

Age range
Five to eleven.

Group size
Whole class.

What you need
An object such as a large shell or a polished pebble which can be passed around the group.

What to do
Children need to develop the skill of taking turns in discussion. This is relatively easy when each child in turn tells the rest of the class about his news or his work. It is much harder when the class is discussing a topic about which all the children have strong opinions they want to voice. They generally find it difficult to listen to each other's contributions. They may all try to speak at the same time or they may fail to listen and respond to what other children have said because they are so keen to put their own points forward and are busy waving their hands to attract attention. Yet it is important that children learn to contribute to this type of discussion by listening and responding.

Possible topics for discussion could include those which are important in the children's lives at school. Examples might be:
• the use of playground space (Does boys' football dominate?);
• school dinners/packed lunches;
• classroom rules and routines;
• where to go on a class outing;
• organisation of the Christmas party.

This activity is designed to stop the children all talking at once and to give more authority to the child who is speaking. The child holds the shell (or other special object) while she is speaking. Only the child holding the shell is allowed to speak.

Children who want to speak will need to indicate, using an agreed signal. (A raised finger is less distracting than a waving hand.) At first you will find it better to pass the shell on to the next speaker yourself. As children gain experience in whole class discussions, the speaker will be able to pass on the shell to a child who indicates that she wants to speak. You will need to ensure, however, that all children have opportunities to speak if they wish and that the shell is not simply passed round among a group of friends.

Closed and open-ended questions

Age range

Five to eleven.

Group size

Whole class or smaller group working in pairs.

What you need

No special requirements.

What to do

Closed questions are those which have a single answer, which is often, though not necessarily, 'yes' or 'no'.
For example:
• What is your name?
• How old are you?
• Where do you live?
• Do you like your job?
   Open-ended questions are those which can lead to a wider range of responses, often involving more thought and reasoning. They cannot generally be answered in a single word. For example:
• Where have you lived in the past?
• What do you like about your job?
• Why did you choose to do that job?
• Have you visited any other countries on holiday?
   When children interview adults they tend to use a great many closed questions and thus get limited information. The following games are designed to help children think about the difference between closed and open-ended questions.

Avoiding 'yes' and 'no'

Children work in pairs and take it in turns to be interviewer and interviewee. The interviewer wins if she succeeds in getting the interviewee to say 'yes' or 'no'. The interviewee has to think of ways to avoid yes/no answers.
For example:

'Did you get any breakfast this morning?'
'I had Sugar Puffs.'
'Do you like Sugar Puffs?'
'I prefer Shreddies.'
...and so on.

The interviewer will need to ask closed questions which require yes/no answers.

Trying to say 'yes' and 'no'

In this game, the interviewee wins if she can reply 'yes' or 'no' to any of the questions asked. The interviewer has to ask questions which will not lead to yes/no answers. For example:

'Why do you like football?'
'Because I like running about and it is fun.'
'How many years have you been playing football?'
'Since I was six, that's four years.'
...and so on.

The children will soon discover that certain question words (Why? What? Who? How?) are very useful in this game because they cannot be answered with a simple 'yes' or 'no'.

Follow-up

Arrange to interview one of the children's parents about his or her job or favourite pastime. This could be done in groups or as a whole class. Children should try to gain as much information as possible by using only open-ended questions. Tape-record the interview and play it back to the children afterwards. Ask them to consider the questions asked and the replies received. Can they think of any ways in which they could improve their questioning techniques?

Questions, questions

Age range

Five to seven.

Group size

Whole class initially; groups of six when children are more competent.

What you need

No special requirements.

What to do

The aim of this activity is to give young children opportunities to ask open-ended questions. It also makes a useful 'time filler' and can help young children begin to understand about interviewing techniques.

Make a statement, such as 'I'm thinking of someone in this class with dark hair'. Invite questions from the class to find out which child it is. Young children will often say, 'Is it Scott?' rather than 'Is it a boy or a girl?' You may need to keep stopping to review the information gained; for example, 'We've discovered that the person is a girl, and she has dark hair and brown eyes. What else do we need to find out about her?' Constantly encourage the children to ask open-ended questions to help them find out information.

Follow-up

Once the children have developed confidence, let them take turns to initiate the game, creating their own starting statements. They could develop the game around objects in the classroom.

The guided tour

Age range
Six to eleven.

Group size
Whole class, then small groups, no more than four children per group.

What you need
Paper, pencils, cassette recorder with a separate microphone, audio cassettes.

What to do
This activity develops skills of organising information in a logical order, and of communicating clearly.

Explain to the children that they are going to make a taped guide for a tour around the school for new parents who come to visit (similar to the taped guides that can be found in museums). As a whole class, brainstorm ideas for the best route around the school and write the ideas on the board. Then, with the children working together in their groups, ask them to arrange all the places which the parents should see in a logical order. Where should the parents go first? When should they visit the 'log trail'? What about the pond?

Once the children in the group have agreed on the order, encourage them to find out as much information as possible about the school, for example:

The school was originally a rectory and was built in the sixteenth century.

This is a new pond which was designed by Year 5. They helped to put in the plants.

Ask them to incorporate their information into a script, and to write a brief introduction to the tour. They should include in the script information about the direction to take, details about each stopping place and indications of where to go next. They should make sure that the directions are clear and easily understood. Rotate the finished instructions so that the groups can read each other's ideas, and test them for clarity.

Once the scripts have been completed, the children can record their tours on to an audio cassette, adding a signal to tell the listener when to turn off the tape and move on to the next place of interest. Let the groups swap cassettes and try out each other's tours, evaluating the effectiveness, and providing necessary feedback.

Follow-up
Use the same idea to make audio cassettes of interest for the local environment or local neighbourhood. Use it as part of a topic on the environment, or on local history.

Instructions

Age range
Seven to eleven.

Group size
Pairs of children.

What you need
Paper, pencils, clipboards.

What to do
This activity encourages precise use of words and careful listening. It will help children learn to give and follow oral instructions.

Ask each child to draw a picture of any everyday object, such as a chair, a spoon or an egg in an eggcup. Tell them that they must not show these drawings to the other children or discuss them.

Arrange the children sitting opposite each other in pairs. They need to rest their paper on clipboards which they tilt up so that their partners cannot see the paper. First, child A gives instructions while child B draws. Child A has to describe her original drawing to child B, using only names of shapes and directions. For example: 'Draw a medium-sized circle in the middle of your paper. Under it, and touching it, draw a square which is slightly larger than the circle...' and so on. Child A should not name the object in the drawing, nor should she use the names of other objects to explain what should be drawn. Child B should try to follow the instructions as precisely as he can. He is not allowed to ask any questions.

When the drawing is complete, child B has to guess what it is intended to represent. They can compare the original version with the one drawn following instructions. Are they different? If so, why? Were the instructions unclear, or were they not followed accurately?

The children then exchange roles. Child B gives instructions to child A to enable her to produce his original drawing.

As the children gain skills in giving and following oral instructions, they will be able to describe more complex drawings.

Follow-up
The children could do similar activities that involve describing routes to be followed on maps, or following instructions to construct a simple LEGO object. (The object will need to be hidden behind a screen so that the child giving instructions cannot see what is happening.)

Note-taking

Age range
Seven to eleven.

Group size
Whole class working individually.

What you need
Videotape of a story, or episodes of the story, a TV and video player, paper and pencils, clipboards.

What to do
Choose a children's story that has been dramatised (make sure that you choose a video that is appropriate for the ages of the children you are working with). Some examples are *The Secret Garden* (BBC Video, 1995), *White Fang* (Walt Disney, 1991), *The Wind in the Willows* (Martin Gates Productions Ltd, 1994) and *The Worst Witch* (Central Independent Television, 1986).

Before you watch the video with the children tell them why it is important to learn to take notes. Explain that it will help them to retain information more clearly, especially if they organise their note-taking under headings. Explain to the children that they are going to watch a video, but that while they watch it you want them to take notes so that they will be able to retell the story accurately at a later date. Give them some headings that you think the children should focus on and that will help them to structure their notes, for example:
- **characters** – to encourage them to list the important people that feature in the story;
- **features** – what particular characteristics characters have, that is, hair colour, height, personality;

CHARACTERS	FEATURES	STORY OUTLINE	PLACES	MAIN POINTS
White Fang	doglike teeth	killed a dog	Alaska	Alaska gold-rush
Jack	kind, nice	Jack found gold in gold mine		
Alex	small, skinny	learnt to read in a hut		Jack robbed
Beauty	male, horrid	mean to W.F. in a field		Jack finds White Fang
Grey Beaver	N. American Indian	tamed W.F. by stream		

- **story outline** – to encourage the children to make brief notes about the story so far, how the action changes and so on;
- **places** – to help the children to situate the story by stating where the action takes place;
- **main points** – to help the children to summarise points that have arisen, issues that need to be followed up and so on.

You may like to present the headings as a grid which the children can then fill in as they watch the video. When the children come to watch the video make sure that they are sitting comfortably and are able to write, using the clipboards, as they watch the programme.

When the children have finally completed their viewing, discuss as a class different children's interpretations through their notes. Give guidance where necessary and encourage the children to support each other while they discuss their ideas. Then ask them to rewrite the story using their notes as guidelines.

Follow-up

Using the same fiction book as the children saw on the video, give each pair of children a photocopy of the first chapter. Explain that this is the section that the children are going to focus on. Give them the same ideas for headings as they used when they watched the video, and let them read the first chapter together. Give the children different coloured highlighter pens. Each colour needs to correspond to a particular heading. Then, on the photocopy, let them use the individual colours to highlight the different categories.

Follow-up questions

Age range

Seven to eleven.

Group size

Whole class.

What you need

Space to sit in a circle.

What to do

Explain to the children that they are going to interview you. Decide together on what the interview should be about, such as what you did at the weekend or during the holidays. Each child will ask a question in turn. Any child who cannot think of a question is allowed to pass. Tell the children that each question they ask must be directly related to your previous answer.

The interview might go like this:

'What did you do in the holidays?'
'I went to Greece.'
'What part of Greece did you visit?'
'Corfu.'
'Why did you choose Corfu?'
'Because it is an island so there are lots of beaches.'
'Do you like beaches?'
'Yes.'
'What do you like about beaches?'
...and so on.

The children will discover that some questions tend to stop the conversation because they produce 'yes' or 'no' answers. These answers may be more difficult to follow up, though

children will soon learn that asking 'Why', 'What' and 'How' questions will produce more information. (See 'Closed and open-ended questions' on page 31.)

Follow-up

Use the same strategy of asking follow-up questions to interview another adult in the school about her work. After the interview, discuss which questions produced the most informative and interesting answers.

Our school

Age range

Five to seven.

Group size

Whole class, then pairs.

What you need

Paper, pens, cassette recorder with separate microphone and blank cassettes.

What to do

In this activity the children are encouraged to decide what they want to find out, to formulate their own questions, and to obtain answers both through observation and through interviewing adults around the school. They will also gain skills in recording, using both writing and tape recording. The school is a secure setting for children to develop and practise these skills.

First discuss with the children what they know about the school and the people who work in it, and what they don't know and would like to find out.

They may not have explored the whole building, particularly in a large school. Have they been inside the junior classrooms, the kitchens or the staff room? With the agreement of colleagues, arrange for small groups of children to make observational visits to these places. On their return, ask them to tell the rest of the class what they saw.

Now discuss what else the children would like to know about their school. Explain to them that they are going to go and interview different people, and they need to decide what they want to find out. For example:

- Where is the secretary's office?
- What does the secretary do with the registers?

- What work does she do on her computer?
- Does she work every day or only some days?
- Is she responsible for the collection and counting of the dinner money and money for school trips?

After the discussion divide the children into pairs and decide which pair is going to interview which member of staff. Ask each pair to think about the questions they will need to ask. Make sure the children write down their questions, so that they can bring them back to the whole class to share ideas. Other children might have suggestions to make that will improve the original ideas.

You will need to check the availability of the members of staff to be interviewed and arrange a convenient time. You will also need to make sure that the children know how to use a portable cassette recorder.

When they are conducting the interviews the children may need to read their questions, but, by working in pairs, one child can read while the other operates the cassette recorder. Check that they take turns to do this.

Follow-up

When they have finished, you could listen to the interviews with each pair and decide which information to keep. Write down the relevant material and either transfer it to a class book, write it out on paper to display alongside a picture of the person interviewed or feed the information into a database programme on the computer (see page 86).

Planning an interview

Age range
Seven to eleven.

Group size
Whole class, later divided into groups.

What you need
Flip chart, paper, pencils, an adult willing to be interviewed.

What to do
Ideally this interview should take place in the context of the current class project. For example, if the children are studying the Second World War they could interview an older person about his life at that time. Another possibility would be to interview someone about her work or about a particular interest or expertise.

Tell the children about the person they are going to interview. As a whole class, brainstorm the areas they would like to ask questions about. For example, if they were interviewing someone about the Second World War the ideas might include: the blitz, food rationing, the blackout, changes at work.

Next divide the class into small groups. Allocate one of these topics to each group and ask them to identify specific areas for questioning. Encourage the children to stick to areas of interest, rather than drawing up a precise list of questions. The drawback with lists of questions is that children tend to be so concerned about asking the next question on their list that they do not listen to the answers they are being given.

Encourage the children to do their interviewing without notes. You could show them a video of a chat show on

television to illustrate this point. Instead of referring to notes, the interviewer usually listens to the response and then follows up what the interviewee has said. It is obvious that research has been done beforehand, but this research has not resulted in a rigid list of questions.

Let each small group interview the visitor separately. Tell them that they will be reporting back to the rest of the class on what they found out. Rather than using a cassette recorder, encourage the children to listen to what is being said and to try to remember what they are told.

After the interview, each group should discuss what they have heard and plan their report back to the class. Encourage them to do this orally, rather than making written notes.

Organising a discussion

Age range
Seven to eleven.

Group size
Whole class.

What you need
Flip chart, pens.

What to do
The purpose of this activity is to offer the children strategies for organising a discussion. Often they switch from one aspect of the topic under discussion to another, and do not focus in depth on anything. This activity can be adapted for use in any class discussion, though it is illustrated here by examples relating to public transport.

Introduce the topic for discussion to the children and let them brainstorm ideas. List all their ideas on the flip chart. It is not always easy to summarise ideas in a few words; ask the children for their suggestions as to exactly what you should write on the flip chart.

For example, if the topic was public transport, you might end up with a list like this:

> - infrequent service
> - lack of leg-room on trains
> - prams and pushchairs
> - long waits
> - too much traffic
> - pollution from large number of cars
> - too many smoking carriages on trains
> - wheelchair users
> - cost
> - blind people
> - not keeping to timetable
> - overcrowding
> - not enough room for shopping on buses

Now help the children organise their ideas into groups or themes. In the list above, there is one theme relating to people who have access problems and may not be able to use public transport, one relating to the timetable (how often the service runs and whether it is on time), one relating to space and facilities on public transport, and one relating to the need for greater use of public transport. List the themes and let the children decide on order of priorities of ideas.

When you are ready to start the discussion, encourage the children to focus in depth on one theme at a time. Sum up the points made about each theme before moving on to a new one. These summaries can be used by the children as a basis for future investigation.

As children grow more used to organising discussions they will be able to identify themes very quickly and suggest an appropriate sequence for tackling them.

Follow-up
Ask the children to use the same techniques to help plan small group discussions. They may find it difficult to note down the brainstormed ideas at first. Make it a rule that each group has a secretary who controls the pace of the discussion.

Workplace expectations

Age range
Five to eleven.

Group size
Whole class.

What you need
Older children may need paper and pencils.

What to do
This activity should take place before a class visit to a workplace. Ask the children what they expect to find out in the course of their visit. What will they see? What sorts of tools or machinery might there be? What jobs will the workers be doing? For younger children this can take the form of a class discussion. Older children will be able to discuss their ideas in groups and list their expectations.

Children's expectations are often very different from reality. For example, a group of nine-year-olds who were about to visit a geriatric hospital expected that work carried out in the hospital would include operations, sex changes and heart transplants! They thought that the 200 workers would nearly all be doctors or nurses.

The process of focusing on expectations means that when the children go on their visit, they are much more alert to the things which do not conform to their expectations. After the visit, ask them what they found out that fitted in with their expectations, and what did not fit in. What were the main differences?

The class who visited the hospital were surprised that there were far fewer doctors than they expected and a wide variety of other workers including physiotherapists, occupational therapists, social workers, laundry workers, porters, administrative staff, a plumber, a carpenter and so on. They were also astonished that the hospital did not have an operating theatre, let alone the highly dramatic operations that they had envisaged.

What can you do about it?

Age range
Five to eleven.

Group size
Whole class, then groups of four.

What you need
Information books, paper, pens, a quiet area for sustained research time, a video recorder and a television.

What to do
This activity is designed to encourage and develop oracy and listening skills in children. It will also help to improve skills of logical thinking so that children may present a clear argument about a particular issue. For older children, the activity will reinforce retrieval skills in order to justify a particular point of view.

Video a debate on television, such as 'Prime Minister's Question Time' or another programme that offers an example of in-depth discussion or debate. After watching this with the children, explain that in a debate people take opposing points of view. Ask two children to take part in a sample debate. One child could argue the case that children should be allowed sweets all day in school, while the other child argues the case that children should not be allowed sweets in school. You need not spend a long time over this; it just gives the children an example of what you are trying to achieve, which is setting up a forum for a controlled debate.

Young children can speak very emotionally about 'recycling' or 'pollution' or the 'ozone layer' but they need to have some facts to argue with. Older children can help younger children to find out the information required; this

also provides an opportunity for two age groups to work together.

For the purpose of beginning a debate, take an issue that is important to the children and one where they can find out firsthand information as well as being given the opportunity to research information. For example, you might want the children to debate the school's surroundings because you are working on a theme about the local environment. The following is an example of a debate that will develop these skills.

Your primary school hall is not big enough to hold all the children in assembly or to provide enough space for gym lessons, nor does it give opportunities for parents to become involved in class assemblies or school functions. The school has put in a bid for major building works for a new school hall and gym.

Organise half the class into groups and ask them to put forward reasons for having a new hall. Organise the remainder of the class into groups of four and get them to put forward reasons against having a new hall. All the groups should list their reasons on paper. Suggest that the latter groups think from the council's point of view

(or whoever will be paying for the new building). They will need to consider whether they have enough money, for example, or whether the new building would spoil the environment around the school.

Older children can carry out research into costs that need to be considered (plans, materials, labour and so on), council meetings, and how permission for plans is granted. All this information will increase the children's knowledge and help them to debate the issue. It is also an issue that is extremely relevant and the skills can be applied in many areas of learning within the school.

Once the children have collated enough information, choose (or let the groups choose) someone confident enough to be able to argue their case. (The groups on each side should pool their information.) You should act as the 'chair' so that you can make final judgements if the debate needs an objective point of view. Set a time limit for the debate – between ten and twenty minutes should be sufficient. Once the two sides of the argument have been offered, open up the debate for comment within the rest of the class. At the end, you need to decide which group has put forward the clearest argument, or you might like the children to vote on it, depending on their maturity.

Follow-up

As far as possible, give children real opportunities for making decisions through the forum of debate. For example, there might be a conflict of use in the school playground. It may be made of Tarmac, the boys being allowed to play football at one end. Use the forum of debate to encourage the children to think of ways in which certain areas could be changed to improve play facilities for all concerned, so that boys and girls may play football, children can sit on benches and so on. Use the debate to present relevant information on which to make decisions and let two classes come together to debate an issue.

Maps for information

Maps are a practical tool used in everyday life. They are also a source of information. Children generally enjoy looking at maps, but they need to develop skills in using them and an understanding of all the information they offer. Children will need to understand about scale and the perspective from which maps are drawn (aerial photographs are helpful in this respect). Using a map involves getting the orientation right and understanding the symbols used. To locate places in atlases and street maps children must be able to use the index, and they will need to understand co-ordinates.

Children should also realise that maps present only a selection of possible information. They need to consider the basis on which that selection was made and to appreciate that maps have limitations: for example, some information will become out of date, and representation of a curved surface in a flat format means that some distortion is inevitable.

Play area map

Age range
Five to seven.

Group size
Whole class, then groups of four.

What you need
LEGO, junk modelling materials, other construction materials, adult helpers to accompany you on a walk if you go to the local play area, paper, pencils, clipboards, baseboards for models.

What to do
Tell the children that you are going to visit a play area, and that you want them to be especially observant on the way there. Point out buildings (including different types of houses – detached, semi-detached, terraced and so on), telephone boxes and anything of interest as you walk along. This is to get the children used to noticing objects that would be on a map. Once at the playground, look at the range of play equipment and encourage the children to notice how the equipment is situated. Draw a simple sketch to remind yourself of everything in the play area.

Back in the classroom, the children can work in groups, with each group using a different construction medium.

Get the children to construct the play area from memory. They will need to discuss how they are going to represent the play equipment, and they will need to negotiate as some will perceive things in different ways.

The finished model maps can be displayed in the classroom. The children could label the various features in their models.

Follow-up
Let the children design a play area of their dreams, using a mapping approach. You could give them a list of appropriate shapes that they could use for slides, swings, a castle and so on.

Classroom map

Age range
Five to seven.

Group size
Whole class, then individuals.

What you need
Paper, pens, a display of maps, boxes and books.

What to do
Ask the children questions about the classroom. What shape is it? How many tables and chairs are there? What other things are important in the classroom? Point out windows, doors and cupboards. Show the children some maps and talk about the fact that maps show things from above, like a 'bird's-eye view'. Using items like boxes and books, on the floor, ask the children to look down on them and to describe what they can actually see, as opposed to what they think the items look like. Explain that the height of

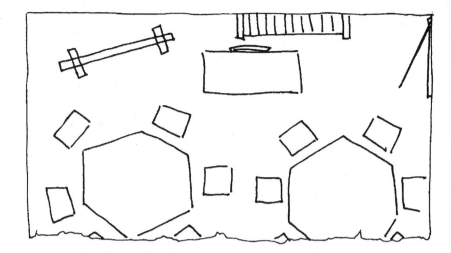

the object does not matter and it is only the size and shape of the base that is relevant.

Now ask the children to draw a map of the classroom from above. Encourage them to think about all the important things previously discussed.

Follow-up
The following activity, 'Using symbols', can be used after this one.

Using symbols

© Crown Copyright

Age range
Five to seven.

Group size
Whole class, then individuals.

What you need
A selection of Ordnance Survey maps, paper, pencils, flip chart, maps of the classroom (see previous activity).

What to do

Talk about how symbols are used in our everyday life. For instance, our writing system is made up of symbols that represent certain sounds. On maps, symbols are pictures that represent things, like wooded areas, churches, railway stations and so on. You could make an enlarged photocopy of a symbol key from an Ordnance Survey map so that the children can see what symbols look like on real maps.

Ask the children to share their classroom maps and discuss whether anybody has attempted to use any kind of symbol. What are the symbols and what are they used for? On a flip chart, you could then draw some appropriate symbols for bookcases, chairs and tables, and let the children make suggestions of their own for other features in the classroom. Encourage them to go back to their maps to see if they can begin to use symbols in them.

Follow-up

Suggest that the children could make maps of their bedrooms at home and bring them in. What symbols will they use? The children could also attempt to map the school building, or the floor where their own classroom is.

Mapping the walk

Age range

Five to seven.

Group size

Whole class working individually or in pairs.

What you need

Adult helpers, selection of Ordnance Survey maps, notebooks and pencils.

What to do

Take your class for a local walk, and encourage them to observe the amenities – houses, trees, shops, anything of interest (the younger the children, the shorter the walk needs to be).

On your return to the classroom, ask the children to map out the journey that they have just taken. Ask them to think of symbols for some of the things they saw on the journey. What could they use to symbolise a tree, or a postbox, for example? What things are important to show on a map, and why? Together, look at examples of different kinds of maps and talk about the symbols used. When they have decided on the symbols they are going to use, suggest that they put them into a 'key'. They might like to have a colour-coded key.

Follow-up

The activity 'The view from above' on page 48 could be used after this one.

The view from above

Age range
Five to seven.

Group size
Four or five children.

What you need
A large-scale aerial photograph of the area around the school (if possible, both an oblique aerial photograph and a vertical one), a large-scale map of the same area (preferably 1:10,000 or, failing that, 1:25,000).

What to do
Ask the group to examine the aerial photograph. Can they recognise anything? If children have not looked at aerial photographs before they may at first find it difficult to work out what they are looking at. Point out the school and the

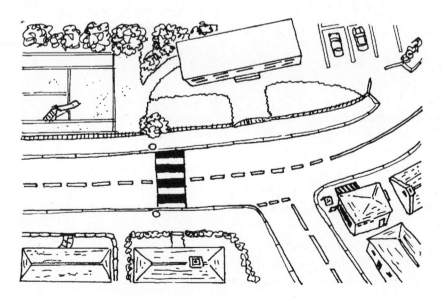

playground. Can the children say where the school entrance is? Once they have got the idea, they are likely to be able to identify other features they recognise such as the zebra crossing, the park, the corner shop.

Oblique aerial photographs are easier to use than vertical ones because they present a more recognisable view, so it may be preferable to start by looking at the oblique photograph, if you have one.

Now introduce the large-scale map or plan of the local area. Children can compare this with the aerial photographs. What information is on the map which is not on the photographs? (Children will find street names particularly useful in finding their way round the map.)

Local maps

Age range
Five to eleven.

Group size
Whole class.

What you need
A display space, a few maps of the local area made for different purposes (for example, bus map, A–Z street plan, Ordnance Survey map), pieces of card.

What to do
Show the children the maps you have collected. How are they different from each other? What purpose was each one made for?

Ask the children to bring in other examples of local maps to add to the display. They could write captions to go with each map explaining what is special about it and suggesting who might want to use it and why.

Encourage younger children to examine and talk about the maps. Older children, working individually or in pairs, could make up questions about one of the local maps. For example:

• What bus do you need to catch to get from the shopping centre to the swimming pool? Which roads would you go on? What would you pass on your way? Which direction would you go in?
• You are in South Street. Where is the nearest Post Office?
• How high is the top of Kite Hill? Is this the highest hill on the map?

Write the questions on cards and pin them around the display. (You may want to add some of your own questions to draw attention to features the children have ignored.) Encourage all the children to look at the maps and find the answers to the questions. After a few days, go through all the questions and answers with the whole class.

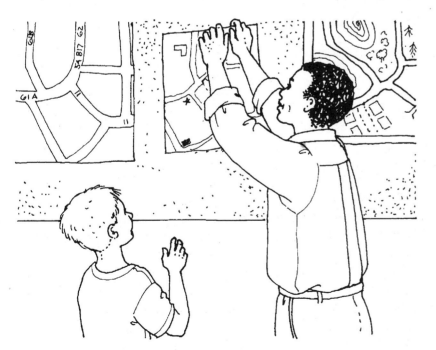

Follow-up

You could ask the children to make their own maps of the area. The following activity, 'Useful maps', can be used.

Useful maps

Age range

Seven to eleven.

Group size

Whole class working in pairs.

What you need

Flip chart, notebooks or paper for planning, large sheets of plain paper, felt-tipped pens, pencils.

What to do

The aim of this activity is to make maps of the local area which will meet the needs of particular users.

Ask the class who they think might need to use local maps. List all their suggestions on a flip chart or board. Suggestions might include:
• a family who have just moved into the area;
• a new bus driver;
• a wholesaler delivering newspapers to shops;
• a new postal worker;
• tourists;
• the fire brigade;
• a blind person who has just moved into the area.

Talk about what sort of information each of these people might need. The family might want to know about facilities such as schools, the park and the doctor's surgery. The wholesaler will need to know where the newsagents' shops are and where it is possible to park. Anyone delivering to houses will need to know exactly where to find each house by name or number, and they might appreciate information about dogs! The fire brigade will need to know the location of fire hydrants, as well as names of streets and locations of houses and businesses. A map for a blind person will need to be constructed from a variety of materials which feel different from each other. It should indicate types of shops and pedestrian crossings.

Ask each pair to select one potential map-user, and list the information that they think that person would need to obtain from a map. Once they have decided what should be included, you will probably need to take the children for a walk round the neighbourhood to collect detailed information.

Before they start to draw their maps remind the children that the map design should take into account the needs of the user. For example, will a small map be easier to use than a larger one? They will need to remember that a blind person will use touch rather than sight to read the map.

Follow-up
Arrange a visit to the local police station or fire station or Tourist Information Office and ask to see the maps that they use for their work.

Co-ordinates and grids

Age range
Seven to eleven.

Group size
Whole class or smaller group.

What you need
A display of maps using different systems of co-ordinates such as A–Z street maps, Ordnance Survey maps and atlases, copies of a page of a street map or photocopiable page 113, squared paper, pencils, felt-tipped pens, copies of photocopiable page 114 (if required).

What to do
Maps use various systems of co-ordinates to enable users to locate specific places. Children need to understand the differences between the various systems and to be able to use each of them.

The simplest system for children to understand is the use of a letter and a number to identify a square on the map. This is the system used in A–Z street maps and most town plans. Explain to the children that, conventionally, letters are used on the x axis and are therefore mentioned first in the reference – A2, E8 and so on. However, children do not need to remember this because there can be no confusion about which square is meant.

Give each child a copy of the street map and ask them to write a list of questions based on the map. For example:

- What is the name of the primary school in B5?
- Which squares include car parks?
- Where is the Information Centre?

The children can then exchange questions with one another and use the map to answer the questions.

Encourage the children to investigate the street maps on display and to set each other challenges which involve using them.

Explain to the class that the system of co-ordinates used on street maps is different from that used on Ordnance Survey maps, where lines rather than spaces are numbered. The advantage of the Ordnance Survey system is that it is possible to locate an exact spot, rather than a square, by using fractions. Children often find it easier to grasp this idea by using vulgar fractions (1½, 2½) rather than decimal fractions (1.5, 2.5). They will need a system for remembering which co-ordinate comes first, such as 'into the house then up the stairs'.

To provide practice in using co-ordinates, give the children squared paper and ask them to draw a map of an imaginary island using this system of co-ordinates (or use photocopiable page 114). Ask them to set questions for other children to answer. You could also ask a group of children to draw a large-scale classroom plan and identify each child's seat by co-ordinates.

Four-figure grid references on an Ordnance Survey map simply involve reading the numbers which label each line. Those at the bottom of the map should be read before those at the side. To pinpoint exact spots, children will need to learn how to use six-figure grid references. They should be

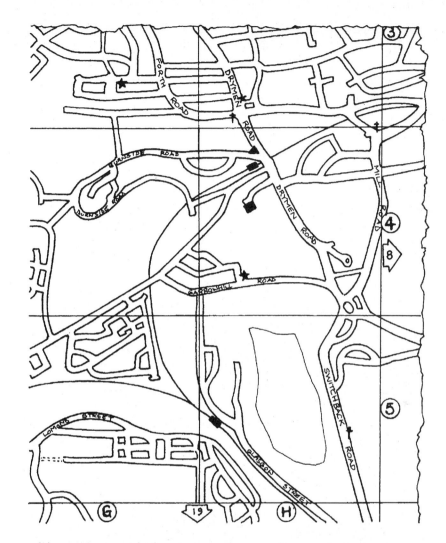

able to cope with these once they understand decimal fractions. A six-figure grid reference includes an additional figure after the number of each line which represents the number of tenths away from that line, thus making it possible to locate a precise spot on the map. To give the children practice in this, you could ask them to identify grid references for various landmarks in the local area.

Orienteering

Age range
Seven to eleven.

Group size
One pair of children at a time.

What you need
Removable adhesive labels, photocopied plans of the room you intend to use (preferably a room which is not in full-time use, for example, the hall, entrance hall, library or television room), an adult helper (to provide extra supervision).

What to do
This activity will require some preparation. First, take about a dozen removable adhesive labels and mark each one with a letter of the alphabet. Then stick the labels around the room. It works better if they are not immediately visible: stick them on the underside of tables or bookshelves, or behind objects on the window-sill. Now mark the positions of the labels on the plan you have prepared, and label each position on the plan with a number from one to twelve. (If you want to make it harder for the children, mark only walls, doors and windows on the plan and omit the furniture.)

Working one pair at a time, the children now have to use the plan to locate each label. Ask them to make a list showing which letter they found at the site of each number on the plan: for example, label C at number 7. Emphasise that they should use the plan to locate the labels, rather than searching for them in a random way.

This activity involves an important map skill – orientation. The child needs to have the plan the same way round as the room in order to be able to use it effectively. That is, if the

door of the room is in front of the child, the plan should be turned so that the door is at the top of the plan.

Follow-up
As the children gain skill in locating labels, use a stopwatch to time how long they take to complete the course. Let each pair set a new course for the next pair, moving the labels and marking a fresh copy of the plan.

Find out whether there is a larger orienteering course nearby. There may be one in a local park where you could take the children to try it out.

Kilometre square

Age range

Seven to eleven.

Group size

Pairs or groups of three.

What you need

Ordnance Survey and other maps of the area around the school on as many different scales as possible (anything from 1:250,000 to 1:1250), paper and pencils.

What to do

Display the maps on a notice-board. Let each pair of children spend some time examining them and comparing the amount of detail shown on each scale. It may be helpful to provide some questions to draw the children's attention to information which is shown on some maps but not others. For example:
• On which of these maps is the school playground large enough to appear in its true shape?
• Which maps show the name of the road the school is in?
• Which maps show the field boundaries?
  On each map, identify the kilometre square in which the school is located. Ask the children to compare the information provided in that square on maps of different scales. Get them to draw up a list indicating how much detail is shown on each map. On which maps are there words written in the square? What other extra information is provided on the larger-scale maps? Encourage children to use the key of the map to find out what the symbols and the different styles of lettering mean.
  On the smaller-scale maps (1:625,000, 1:250,000, 1:125,000) they could compare the 10 kilometre square around the school.

Follow-up

Discuss what the different scale maps would be used for. Which one would be most useful for holiday-makers? What scale would be best for a walker? What about motorists and cyclists?

Scale and distance

Age range

Seven to eleven.

Group size

Pairs of children.

What you need

A display of maps, including Ordnance Survey maps of the area around the school (a large scale plan at 1:2500 or 1:1250 and a 1:50,000 map), a map of the British Isles and a world map (all should have the scale clearly marked), string, clothes pegs, paper and pencils.

What to do

Explain to the children how the linear scale shown on each of the maps can be used. Demonstrate how the distance between two places on the map can be measured using a piece of string. (The simplest way to do this is to cut the string to the exact length needed for the distance. However, this uses rather a lot of string; an alternative is to mark the end of the distance on the string using a clothes peg.) The string is then laid along the linear scale and the distance read off. If the distance is longer than that shown on the scale, they will need to measure the string in sections. The advantage of using string rather than paper strips is that distances can be measured along roads and paths, rather than simply in a straight line.

Once the children have grasped the idea, encourage them to measure distances on the various maps provided. They could measure the distance from home to school, to the nearest town, to the seaside, from one town to another. Ask them to write down their findings. They will need to state whether they have measured as the crow flies, or whether they have followed roads. (They could measure the same journey in both ways and see how much further it is for a car than a crow!)

Follow-up

Children could make plans of the classroom on different scales: 1 centimetre represents 1 metre (1:100); 1 centimetre represents 50 centimetres (1:50); 1 centimetre represents 10 centimetres (1:10). This will probably be the largest scale you want to attempt: the plan will be about 1 metre square. Get the children to measure and mark on the plan all the furniture.

How up to date are maps?

Age range
Seven to eleven.

Group size
Groups of three or four children.

What you need
A large-scale Ordnance Survey map or a plan of the area around the school (1:10,000 or preferably 1:2500 or 1:1250), a large-scale aerial photograph of the same area (blown up as large as possible).

What to do
Ask the children to compare the map and the photograph. Can they list any features which are shown on the map but are not on the photograph, and vice versa? Which do they think was produced first – the map or the photograph? Children should be able to work this out from their own knowledge of the area as it is today.

It is probable that the photograph will be much more recent than the map. Map surveying is a slow and laborious task. Even when Ordnance Survey maps are updated it is often only the main roads and major features that are changed; indications of buildings and field boundaries usually remain as they were when the map was first produced, often decades ago. A note of when it was last updated will be printed on the map.

Can the children work out how long ago the photograph was taken? Has the area changed in any way since then? For instance, have new buildings been built since the photograph was taken? You may need to take the children for a walk round the area to spot the changes.

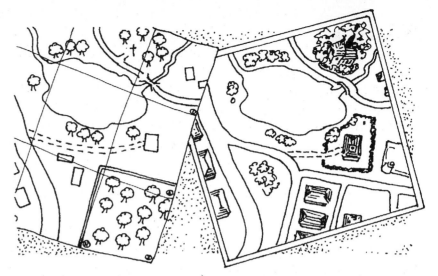

Discuss how important it is to have up-to-date maps. Who uses maps? What sort of information do they need? How quickly does the landscape change? (Children's ideas about this will vary. Those who live near a newly built motorway, for example, will realise that dramatic change can take place quite quickly. Children who live in areas where there has been relatively little change may not realise how much the landscape can change in a short time.)

Great circle routes

Age range
Seven to eleven.

Group size
Pairs or groups of three.

What you need
A globe, copies of a world map, such as the one on photocopiable page 115 (Mercator's projection), string, Blu-Tack, airline magazines or timetables showing routes used.

What to do

Help the children to mark London, Vancouver and Tokyo on their copy of the world map. Ask them to draw the shortest route for an aeroplane to fly between London and Vancouver, and between London and Tokyo.

Now help the children to locate London, Vancouver and Tokyo on the globe. Use string to find the shortest route between London and Vancouver, and between London and Tokyo. (The routes will go across the Arctic.) Fix the string to the globe using Blu-Tack. These routes are called 'great circle routes'.

Ask the children to compare the routes they marked on the world map with the routes marked on the globe. What places does each route fly over? Where does it cross the coast? Why are the two routes different? Now ask them to transfer the great circle routes marked on the globe on to their maps. Why do these routes not appear as straight lines on the map? Point out that the map always distorts reality because it is not possible to represent a sphere on flat paper. The globe is the more accurate way of representing the world.

In order to find which route is the shorter, the children will need to make a direct comparison on the globe by fixing a second piece of string to mark the 'straight line route' from the map. The piece of string marking the great circle route will be shorter.

Follow-up

Compare the routes identified with those shown in the airline literature. Do aeroplanes always use the shortest routes? What reasons might there be for diverging from the shortest route? Possible reasons would include flying with the prevailing winds, avoiding bad weather and war zones, the need to refuel, avoiding areas where there are few radio beacons to aid navigation, and the difficulty of flying on a constantly changing compass bearing. The main reason is traffic congestion; few flights within Europe go by the most direct routes.

How big is Greenland?

Age range

Nine to eleven.

Group size

Pairs or small groups.

What you need

A globe, atlases and world maps using different projections (Mercator's, Peters, and a projection in which lines of longitude are shown curved, such as Mollweide's or Aitoff's), or copies of the maps on photocopiable pages 115–117.

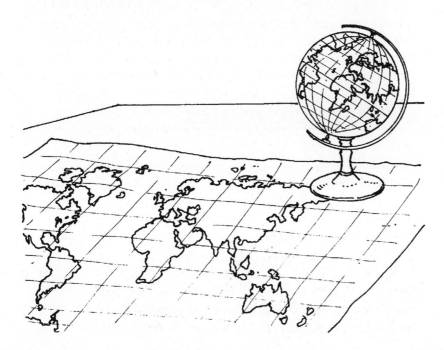

What to do

Examine the various maps together. Ask the children to compare the size of Africa and Greenland on Mercator's projection. They will see that they are about the same size. Now ask them to look at the same areas on Aitoff's projection. Greenland appears tiny in relation to Africa. Next examine Peters projection. How do the relative sizes appear on this one? Make similar comparisons between other areas on the map – for example, Europe and South America, Canada and the USA.

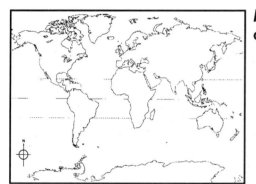

Mercator's Map of the World

Aitoff's Map of the World

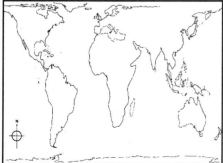

Peters Map of the World

Explain to the children that it is very difficult to represent the world on a flat sheet of paper because it is actually a sphere. The globe is the most accurate way of representing the world. Ask the children to look on the globe at the relative sizes of the countries and areas they have been comparing.

Discuss which of the map projections is the most accurate in portraying the size of each area. The Peters projection was specifically designed to represent relative size accurately. Projections with curved lines of longitude also show size reasonably accurately.

Next ask the children to examine the shapes of Africa and Greenland on each map and on the globe. Discuss which projection represents shapes most faithfully. All map projections distort the shapes of some countries. Mercator's has the least distortion. Which countries are shown with the greatest distortions? On most projections shapes are shown accurately around the Equator, while shapes around the North and South Poles are distorted. This is particularly noticeable when focusing on the shape of Greenland. However, on the Peters projection, the most accurate shapes are those at the 45 degree lines of latitude. In this projection countries around the Equator are distorted, so Africa appears very long and thin.

Discuss with the children the relative advantages and disadvantages of each projection.

Follow-up

You could go on to compare how the different map projections show direction. What compass direction would you have to follow to go from Newfoundland to Iceland, or from Brazil to Greenland? The advantage of Mercator's projection is that compass bearings are generally accurate. Maps with curved lines of longitude distort direction. On the Peters projection East and West are shown accurately, but a direction such as North-west is not.

Media sources

The media play a significant role in children's daily lives. The influence of television on children's behaviour is a constant source of debate. There is no doubt that the media influence children's choices and decisions; it is of great importance, therefore, that children learn about the techniques used by the media so that they may be encouraged to make more objective decisions.

Younger children are particularly susceptible to the marketing media and are easily swayed by advertisements for certain products or the 'cult' toy of the moment. It is important for you as the teacher to be aware that they will need considerable support, guidance and continuous interaction in order to gain some knowledge and learn about some of the techniques used in advertising. By studying, and where possible, analysing, the techniques used within the media, we offer children the opportunity to take more control over their own lives and choices.

Television advertisements

Age range
Five to eleven.

Group size
Whole class, then groups of four.

What you need
A television and video recorder, photocopiable page 118, videotape of television advertisements. (Choose two or three that are likely to be shown on Saturday mornings or early evening, during children's television. Be selective in order to show different products, for example a toy and a food product.)

What to do
Show the video of the television adverts to the children. Lead a general discussion about advertising, and draw the children's attention to the target audiences for different advertising campaigns. For example, ask them why we have adverts. One reason is that independent television companies need the money they receive from advertising to run their companies, since they do not receive money from the government as the BBC does. What is the purpose of adverts? Do they encourage you to buy certain goods even though you may not really need what is being advertised? Is that how adverts achieve their aims?

Once you have raised the children's awareness of these issues, group them into fours and appoint one child as the scribe or secretary. Ask the children to discuss the advertisements and the questions you have raised. Tell them that they are going to report back their findings to the whole class. You might like to put the following questions on a sheet for each group to guide the children's discussions.

- Why do we have advertisements?
- What did you notice about the adverts that you have watched? What were they trying to achieve?
- How do the adverts try to persuade people to buy their products? List some things that you noticed from the adverts you have just seen.
- How do advertisers show that the product is aimed at boys or girls? Is this important?
- How much do you think is spent on advertising? Do you think it is worth the expense?
- Do people take notice of adverts and do adverts really influence their lives?

When you think the groups have spent long enough on their discussions, bring the children back together and ask each scribe to share the group's ideas with the rest of the class. Then look at the video again, stopping at important points raised by the children in their discussions.

Now ask the children to go back into their groups and give each group one advert to focus upon. Give them a copy of photocopiable page 118 and ask them to discuss

the questions. Alternatively, you may like to make up your own questions suited to your class and their needs. The children will need to analyse the product on offer and will need to write down their answers to the questions on a large sheet of paper. They will need to discuss how they can arrange their information: it could be in the form of a chart, or simply in list form, or they could feed it into a database system (see page 86). It is important that the children make their own decision about the format.

Follow-up
When children watch television at home, encourage them to ask questions for themselves about the adverts. This will engender open-ended enquiry which will continue and develop. It is also important to raise issues of stereotyping and bias, which older children will enjoy debating at length. You may like to give the children a copy of photocopiable page 118 to fill in as they watch the television.

Adverts in magazines and comics

Age range
Five to eleven.

Group size
Whole class, then small groups.

What you need
Multiple copies from a good selection of children's comics and magazines, copies of the *Radio Times*, *TV Times*, and other popular magazines and papers generally found at home, scissors, paper, pencils, pens.

What to do

Let the children look through the magazines and comics and select a variety of adverts, if possible choosing ones that advertise similar products, for example bathroom cleaners, toothpastes, cars, or diet food products. (You will need to help younger children choose carefully because they may not understand the wider concepts involved in diet food products, though they may be persuaded by chocolate or ice-cream adverts!)

Divide the children into groups and ask them to cut out the adverts and sort them into the categories. Younger children can talk about the differences in the products by describing the pictures in the adverts and by identifying the products. They can talk about the images used in advertising cars or make-up products, for example, and in their groups can write up their findings either individually or as a whole group.

Older children can be encouraged to analyse the thoughts behind the images. Some adverts have powerful images which need to be discussed carefully. Talk the children through this, as it is not easy. Younger children

especially take so much on face value. They believe literally what the advert is saying: for instance, if the diet drink suggests that inches will be lost then that is often what they believe.

Ask the children to write down what they actually see in the picture. They should list all the items that they think are important and then say why they are important. Older children can then begin to analyse how the advertisers manipulate the public. In groups, get the children to talk about and discuss the pictures. Have they noticed similar things about the pictures? Then let them individually write a description of the picture. Get them to think how far the image relates to the wording of the advert. Then ask them to write an analysis of the whole advert, including an assessment of what the image is portraying and how the text is linked. Try to encourage them to have a personal view about what the image really means to them.

Follow-up

Share the ideas and findings of different children, either in small groups or as a whole class. Older children can attempt a debate upon the ethics of some advertising campaigns.

Making your own TV advert

Age range

Five to seven.

Group size

Whole class, then groups of six.

What you need

A large space.

After the children have presented their adverts, discuss as a whole class which group managed to persuade the audience that their product was worth buying. In the discussion try to analyse how they achieved this success.

The more experienced the children become at exploring drama and improvisation, the better they will be able to invent their own stories and use their imagination. They should then be able to develop their own scenarios for advertising whatever products they choose.

Follow-up
Encourage the children to write down the script for their advert, so that they may repeat their work on another day and as they do so try to improve on their achievements.

Video adverts

Age range
Seven to eleven.

Group size
Groups of between six and eight.

What you need
A large space, notebooks and pencils, a video camera.

What to do
Drawing upon previous work on advertising styles, ask the children to develop and improvise their own adverts for a particular product of their own choice. Divide them into groups and ask them first to discuss their ideas, then to develop their ideas into a cohesive order, and finally to act them out.

What to do
Drawing on the knowledge that the children have built up on styles of advertising, talk with the class about dramatising an advert that they have seen on children's TV. Select an advert that everyone knows well – it could be an advert for sweets, perhaps – and suggest to a group of children that they improvise the actions while you talk through the advert. The rest of the children should act as an audience, listening and watching carefully. The younger the children are, the less experienced they will be in exploring drama work, so you will need to choose a fairly simple advertisement.

Divide the children into groups and ask them to talk about the advert that they want to act out. Move around the groups, giving assistance and making sure that there is a variety of adverts and products being dramatised. (You will need to allow very young children to enact an advert they know well.) Then let each group act out their advert to the rest of the class.

You should move around the groups, giving support and encouragement where necessary. Help each group to make notes about the story-line and whether there will be different scenes involved. Encourage them to rehearse and refine their ideas, and to write scripts of their work in their notebooks. This will probably be time-consuming, and they will need your support, particularly if they want to include music as part of the performance. When they are ready, ask each group to present their ideas to the remaining groups.

After the first performance by all the groups, discuss whether they have been able to incorporate bias and persuasion into their production. Talk about ways in which they could make their advert more effective. You could consider the ways in which some advertisers use famous people to help sell their products.

When they (and you) are satisfied with their finished products, make a video recording of each one. The video camera could either be set up on a stand (which is much easier to manipulate) or you could use a hand-held camera. Again, the maturity of the children will help you decide whether to allow them to use the camera and film for themselves or whether to do it for them.

Follow-up

Show the finished results to another class and discuss how effective the adverts are. Do they really encourage and persuade the viewer to buy the product?

Making a class newspaper

Age range
Five to seven.

Group size
Whole class working in self-selected groups.

What you need
A selection of newspapers/children's newspapers (for example, *Young Telegraph*)/local papers/comics (which the children can recognise), paper, pencils, pens, scissors, glue, stapler, cassette recorder, blank tapes.

What to do
Read a few articles from the paper to the children. Choose items that will be of particular interest to them. You could begin with the sports reports, or an item about animals. Display various news reports to give the children an idea of different styles of writing.

Tell the children that you want to produce your own class newspaper about things that are happening around them and discuss with them any important events in their lives or the school's life. One of the children might have a new baby brother or sister, for example. You could make a special column for that information. Some children might play in netball or football teams or have older brothers or sisters who do so. Encourage those children to talk about recent matches. Other children might have very specific interests that they wish to share. They might have seen a film or a video or read a book that they want to recommend. All these things provide an ideal opportunity for children to work together on their own news stories.

Some of the younger children will have difficulty writing for themselves, so it is a good idea to pair such children with a more competent child, or even to suggest that they record their ideas on a cassette recorder and you can be the scribe. All the children will be able to draw something and possibly write a caption underneath. Also remind the children that most papers include a quiz section, puzzles and a joke or cartoon corner.

As a whole class, decide on the size of 'newspaper' that you want to produce. Appoint an 'editorial' group of three or four children who are good readers. Help this group to sort the stories or pieces of work into categories and then to arrange and paste the articles on to the pages of the newspaper. You will need to point out to the children that they should look at the length of the stories and see whether any will have to be adapted for the paper. If the children are very young the work can be done in their own handwriting, although older children who are more conversant with the word processor could use that for their writing.

When all the pages are complete, photocopy and staple together enough copies for each child in the class, with a few extra for the class and school libraries. You could try selling further copies to cover the cost of paper and photocopying.

Follow-up
If the venture is a success, you could repeat it every month or two months. You could also include interviews with members of staff.

Making a school magazine

Age range
Seven to eleven.

Group size
Whole class, then groups of four.

What you need
A selection of quality general magazines (including Sunday newspaper magazines), paper, pencils, pens, stapler or spiral binder, access to a computer and printer.

What to do

Choose similar types of articles from three different magazines to read to the children. These could be a report on an environmental issue, a review of a play or a book, an advice column or a features item about the 'royals'. Talk about the styles of writing and how the writers approach the topic. What techniques do the writers use to gain the readers' interest? Point out the importance of getting the message across in a clear and concise way. Journalistic writing has to be brief and to the point because there is often a space limit placed on articles.

Tell the children that you would like them to produce a school magazine. Divide them into groups of four and ask them to consider the contents of the magazine. What article types do they want to include? What sort of features do they wish to include? Let the children have access to the magazines so that they can use them as models. After about 15 minutes, stop the group discussions and bring the class together to find out what decisions different groups have made.

Next, give each group a particular section to write. These could include: a review section on books, films, TV programmes, videos and music; a sports section; a fashion section; a features section; a puzzle section with jokes, crosswords and competitions; a school news section; a 'pictures' (photographs) section. You could also put one group in charge of marketing, asking them to design adverts or to devise ways of encouraging people to advertise in the magazine. Another group can design the overall layout of the magazine and the front cover and contents page. Make one person in each group the 'editor' who has the final say about which items should be included. Help the children to think about the length of their articles and how they can put across all the information using the minimum number of words. (Some children will be thrilled to do this, especially if they find writing an arduous

task!) Encourage the groups to work collaboratively, checking one another's spelling, grammar and punctuation. (You might need to check this too if the magazine is to be sold around the school.)

When the articles are ready for typing, help each group to type their reports on the word processor, using columns. Make sure that each child has a turn at typing. Encourage the children to think about the type size and whether a change of font is necessary for certain items. The headlines will need to be in a larger size and probably in bold type.

Finally, cut out and paste the reports on to the pages of the magazine, then photocopy and staple or bind it together. Remember to decide on a suitable name for the magazine.

Follow-up

Make enough copies to sell to other classes in the school. If you manage to sell enough copies and make a profit, then the class can decide how the money should be spent! You could also ask for items from children in other classes, and perhaps an article from the headteacher or other members of staff. You may well decide to produce the magazine monthly or termly, depending on the response.

Designing an advert

Age range
Five to eleven.

Group size
Pairs or individuals.

What you need
Paper, pens, pencils, large and small felt-tipped pens, poster paints, a range of newspaper and magazine adverts, *The Jolly Postman or Other People's Letters* by Janet and Allan Ahlberg (Heinemann, 1995), *Willy the Wimp* by Anthony Browne (Walker Books, 1995).

What to do
Look through the newspapers and magazines with the children to gain ideas about how adverts are designed. Tell the children that you want them to design their own adverts and help them to decide what it is they want to advertise. What sort of a product will it be? It can be a made-up one or a familiar one. It need not be a serious advert. Draw

their attention to the adverts in *Jolly Postman* and *Willy the Wimp*. Both include humour in their illustrations, which older children may be able to draw upon when designing their own adverts.

Tell the children to plan their designs carefully. They should think of the most effective wording. Are short, sharp phrases better than long sentences? Encourage them to try out colour tones. What is it that makes the impact – the colour, the design or the words used? Ask them to share with a friend to see how effective their designs are.

When they are satisfied with their designs, they should make final versions which can then be displayed around the class or school. Some of them could be reduced and included in a class newspaper.

Follow-up
Look at the variety of small ads that appear in local newspapers. Explain to the children that newspapers charge according to how many words are used in each ad and therefore it is very important when writing an advert to choose each word carefully. Give each child a copy of photocopiable page 119 and ask them to compose their own small advert.

Television news

Age range
Five to eleven.

Group size
Whole class in groups of five or six.

What you need
No special requirements.

What to do

Divide the class into groups and draw up a rota so that each week one group is responsible for presenting a 'TV programme' of school and class news and events to the rest of the class. For older children this programme should have a fixed time slot and length – say, fifteen minutes.

The programme should be presented in a television news format, so the children will need to watch the news on television beforehand to get ideas about presentation. They will need to take on the roles of newsreaders, interviewers, reporters at the scene and so on. They may also want to interview other children who are not part of the group.

The whole group will need to act as researchers, finding out what has happened that week. They have to fill their programme even if there is very little news. Thus they may need to resort to trivia: for example, 'Gina's kittens opened their eyes'; 'Sean bought a new jumper.' Other weeks may present an abundance of news items, such as a football match, a class outing, particularly bad weather. In this case the children will need to select what should be included and what should be left out.

The presentation of the news should include interviews and on-scene reports, just as the news on television does.

Live broadcast

Age range

Seven to eleven.

Group size

Four to six children, or whole class working in groups.

What you need

Access to a range of information books relating to the historical topic that will be the subject of a live broadcast; a hand-held microphone, a cardboard television screen frame.

What to do

This activity provides a way of encouraging children to use information in books for their own purposes, rather than copying from them directly. It should also help bring historical events to life, so that they have more reality for the children.

Ask the children to choose a particular historical event from the period they are studying: this might be the Norman invasion or the Great Exhibition. The whole class could be involved in this activity by having groups working on different events in the same period, for example the Battle of Edge Hill, the Restoration, the Great Plague and the Great Fire of London. Ask the children to prepare and present a 'live' television broadcast about this event.

They will need to use reference books and encyclopaedias to find out as much as they can about the event. (If they choose an event in living memory, such as the coronation of Queen Elizabeth II, they will also be able to gain information from adults who were alive at the time.) They will need to decide what are the most important facts and issues in relation to the event.

The children also need to watch news and current affairs programmes on television and to study the way in which they are presented. Usually there are headlines followed by a more detailed account of each event, including reporters interviewing witnesses and participants at the scene, and sometimes studio interviews about issues and controversies. The children will need to allocate roles for their presentation – news presenter, reporter at the scene, various people to be interviewed. The group will need time to plan and rehearse their broadcast.

Finally, they can present their programme to the rest of the class or to the whole school in assembly.

Headline news

Age range
Seven to eleven.

Group size
Whole class working in pairs, then individually.

What you need
Newspapers or collection of stories cut out of newspapers, separate collection of headlines from newspapers (for example, 'Man mauled by tiger', 'Vanishing bride mystery', 'Puzzling letter from America' and so on) or use the examples supplied on photocopiable page 120.

What to do
Give each pair of children a newspaper story to read. Ask them to look at the order in which the story is told and the ways in which journalists select and use words to make the story sound interesting and dramatic. Styles that might be encountered include such phrases as: 'scientists have found a real-life Jurassic Park'; 'soaraway success'; 'the victim of a hate campaign'. A common stylistic device in newspapers is the way in which people are described: 'the 28-year-old former Commonwealth Games 800-metre gold medallist'; or '35-year-old blonde mother-of-five, Mary Smith'. The children should also consider whether the headline is successful in grabbing the reader's attention.

Bring the whole class together to talk about their findings and share examples of journalistic style. How do journalists try to attract the reader's attention? Do all newspapers use the same style?

Now give each child a newspaper headline, without the relevant story. Ask the children to write a story based on their headline, using the same style as journalists and making it sound as exciting as possible.

Be a critic

Age range
Seven to eleven.

Group size
Small groups.

What you need
Paper, pencils.

What you do
Brainstorm with the children a list of television programmes that they watch during the week and at weekends, and write this on the board so that everyone can see. Ask the children to choose their favourite three programmes from the list. Discuss with the children why they chose those particular programmes. Were they interesting, entertaining, educational? What do they think makes a 'good' or 'bad' television programme? Ask them to write down their views once they have discussed them.

Using a simple show of hands, get the children to vote for their three favourite programmes. Put the names of the most popular programmes on the board and ask all the children to make a point of watching those particular TV programmes during that week, if their parents agree.

For each of these programmes they should answer the following questions:
• What is the title of the programme?
• Name three things that you liked about the programme.
• Name three things that you did not like about it.

Having watched all three programmes they should finally decide which programme they liked best and why.

The following week, invite the children to discuss their evaluations in class, helping them to focus on the critical factors of their analysis. Recap on what they decided were the important features of a good TV programme. Ask them to read out their critiques to each other and discuss the various points of view which may emerge. Encourage the children to look more critically at programmes in the future.

Follow-up
Challenge the children to design their own television programmes based on the criteria set for a 'good' TV programme. They can perform these to each other or to the rest of the class and they can critique each other's characterisations, choice of music and so on.

Numerical data

The need for children to be able to represent numerical data in tables and graphs, and to be able to interpret such data, is emphasised in several curriculum areas: mathematics, information technology, science, geography.

We are presented with a wide range of figures and statistics in daily life through the media, when we go shopping and so on. Data can be used to mislead and to persuade, as well as to inform. Children need to develop skills which will not only help them to understand the statistics they are presented with, but also to evaluate them critically. They can also learn how to use figures to support their own arguments.

Weather reports

Age range
Seven to eleven.

Group size
A group of about ten children, working in pairs.

What you need
Photocopies of reports on the previous day's weather in different parts of the British Isles and around the world (provided in many daily papers), world atlases and road atlases of the UK, copies of a map of the British Isles (such as the one on page 121), copies of a world map (such as the one on page 122 – you could also use those needed for the activities 'Great circle routes' and 'How big is Greenland?'), squared paper, pencils, felt-tipped pens.

What to do
Give each pair of children copies of the weather reports and tell them to focus on a particular aspect of the data, such as temperatures around the world, rainfall in the UK or hours of sunshine in the UK. Tell them first to rearrange the data in numerical order from greatest to least. For example, one pair may list cities around the world in order of temperature, from highest to lowest. (A word processor would make this task easier.) Once the list is in order, the data can be displayed as a bar graph.

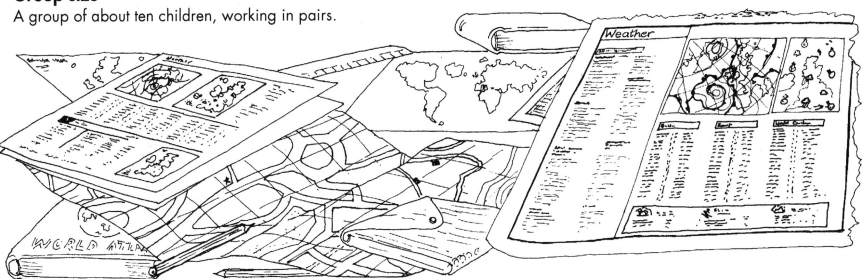

Tell the children to use the index of the atlas (world or UK) to locate the different towns and cities listed, and then to mark them on a blank map. (Give them the relevant photocopiable map.) The aim now is for each group to show their data on a map, so that spatial patterns can be investigated. One way to do this is by using a colour coding system. For example, temperatures on a world map could be indicated by marking cities with different coloured spots:

- over 30 degrees – red;
- 20–29 degrees – orange;
- 10–19 degrees – yellow;
- 0–9 degrees – pale blue;
- sub-zero – dark blue.

Once all the places are marked on the world map, it will be possible to see some sort of pattern. Where are the hottest places? Where are the coldest? Why are some places hotter than others? (Reasons include the fact that some are nearer the Equator, temperatures are affected by seasonal change.)

Similar scales could be worked out for amounts of rainfall, hours of sunshine and temperatures in the UK. The range in temperature will be much smaller in the UK than over the whole world, so a different colour scale will need to be devised.

Follow-up

A different group could undertake the same activity one or two weeks later, and then compare their display with that of the previous group. What differences are there between the graphs and maps? Is the weather pattern similar or has it changed?

Repeat the activity again several months later. There are likely to be more noticeable differences in findings over a longer period, as seasons change.

Children could investigate the climate maps in atlases and compare these with their own findings.

Transport timeline

Age range
Seven to eleven.

Group size
Whole class, then groups of four.

What you need
Flip chart and pen, a range of information books (including books about the history of transport, Victorian times and the twentieth century), encyclopaedias, a piece of string across the classroom well above head height, clothes pegs, A4 paper, felt-tipped pens.

The First Plane Flies! 1903

Once the children have carried out their research tell them to make a poster for each significant date. The date and the event should be written boldly as a headline, with more details, or an illustration, underneath. Once all the posters have been completed they can be attached to the line with clothes pegs, in the correct chronological order.

Follow-up
Ask the children to find out more about what it was like to travel at different times. See also 'Journey 1850' on page 26.

Favourite dinners

Age range
Five to eleven.

Group size
Whole class.

What you need
Paper, pencils, squared paper or graph paper (for older juniors), felt-tipped pens, computer with word-processing program and data-processing program, photocopying facilities.

What to do
As a class, discuss children's feelings about school dinners. Use the results of this discussion as a basis for devising a questionnaire to find out the opinions of other children in the school. Questions could include such matters as likes and dislikes, menus, choices offered, helping size, service system, time allowed to eat. Decide whether a multiple-choice questionnaire would be suitable or whether it would

What to do
Explain to the children that they are going to find out when the major developments in the history of transport took place. Ask them what sort of events would be included. They might suggest the first car, the first aeroplane, the first train and so on.

Ask the children when they think each of these inventions was made. In what order were the main forms of transport invented? Then encourage them to think of more specific categories, such as the first aeroplane to fly, the first aeroplane to cross the Channel, the first aeroplane to carry passengers and so on.

List all their suggestions on a flip chart. Then divide the children into smaller groups and allocate to each group an aspect of the history of transport to research, using the suggestions on the flip chart. It will probably be better if the groups do their research at different times since they may need to use the same books.

be more useful to give children space to write their own ideas. How will the questionnaire be administered? Can it be given out to children to complete themselves, or does an interviewer need to be present to help children read the questions and fill in their responses? Should every child in the school have a chance to respond, or just a sample of children? What about children who do not eat school dinners? Should their opinions be sought?

Once the questions have been agreed, the children can take it in turns to word-process them. The final questionnaire will need to be photocopied, and then distributed in the way the children have decided.

When all the questionnaires have been returned, responses to each question will need to be analysed. You could get a small group of children to take responsibility for each question. The findings could be presented in the form of tables and graphs, or you could use a data-processing program on the computer to help analyse and present the findings.

The results of this activity should enable the children to identify aspects of schools dinners with which most people are satisfied, and aspects which might be changed.

You might like to invite the cook to visit the classroom and let the children tell her about their findings. They could also prepare a written report setting out all their findings for her to take away. As a result of this she may be able to take some of the children's views into account in future menus. She is also likely to respond with reasons why some current practices cannot be changed. These in turn should be conveyed to the rest of the school, perhaps in an assembly.

Low-fat products?

Age range
Nine to eleven.

Group size
Whole class working in groups of four.

What you need
Paper, felt-tipped pens, a collection of food packages including some which claim that the products are 'healthy' in some way (for example low fat, low sugar, low salt, high fibre), and packages of similar foods which do not make health claims. (Ask the children to bring these packages in several days beforehand.)

What to do
Give each group packages of a particular type of food, including some that make health claims and some that do not. For example, one group could have yoghurt and fromage frais cartons, some of which claim to be low-fat products.

Ask the children to look at the nutritional information on each package. They need to use the table which indicates how many grams of protein, carbohydrate, fat and so on are contained in each 100 grams of the product. They should then list all the brands they have, showing how many grams of fat there are in each one. Ask them to make a bar chart showing all the products in order of fat content and using a different colour for the bars representing 'low-fat' products.

Do the 'low-fat' products have the lowest fat content? What percentage of fat is 'low'? How does the fat content of a low-fat spread compare with that of a low-fat yoghurt?

Follow-up
This information could be presented in the form of pie charts using a computer.

Discuss why food manufacturers claim that their products are low in fat, sugar and salt, and high in fibre. How is this related to health?

Multiples of ten

Age range
Seven to eleven.

Group size
Pairs or individuals.

What you need
Atlases, local maps on different scales, encyclopaedias, metre rule, trundle wheel, photocopiable page 123.

What to do
Large numbers are very difficult to comprehend. This activity is designed to give children some realistic idea of what they mean.

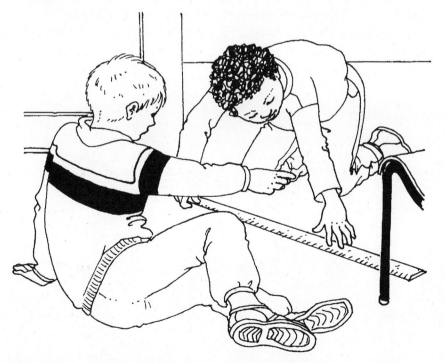

Give each child or pair a copy of the photocopiable sheet and ask them to fill in the blanks. This will need to be tackled in different ways. Measuring on the ground will locate objects one, ten and possibly 100 metres away. A large-scale map will be needed to find out what is one kilometre away. Smaller-scale maps and globes will be needed to investigate larger distances, and encyclopaedias will prove necessary for very large distances.

Some children will enjoy continuing this exercise beyond the bounds of the Earth. For example, 100,000 kilometres is a quarter of the distance to the Moon!

Traffic survey

Age range
Five to eleven.

Group size
Groups of up to six children.

What you need
Clipboards, pencils, a dry day, a safe place from which to observe traffic, plenty of adult helpers.

What to do
A traffic survey provides children with the opportunity to collect and analyse numerical data. However, it should not be simply an artificial exercise. It is important that the survey has a purpose and that the children use the data they have collected. The purpose of surveying traffic could be to produce evidence:
• to back calls for a pedestrian crossing or for a crossing warden;
• to be used in a debate about the need for traffic calming

measures or a bypass to relieve traffic congestion;
• as part of an investigation about air and noise pollution;
• as part of a joint project with another school in a contrasting environment.

The purpose of the survey will determine what data needs to be collected.

Discuss with the children whether they need to know:
• the total number of vehicles;
• separate totals for each direction;
• numbers of vehicles of different types: cars, lorries, bicycles, buses and so on;
• the place of origin of each vehicle (which can be determined from the number plate);
• types of goods being transported in lorries;
• numbers of pedestrians.

The children will also need to decide what time of day the survey should be carried out, and whether it should be repeated. Ten or fifteen minutes is an adequate time span for recording (less on a very busy road).

Ideally the survey should be carried out from a safe location such as the playground. Parental permission should be obtained if the children are going outside the school grounds. If it is necessary to stand on the pavement, the groups of children should be very small and each group should be accompanied by an adult.

Before going out, show the children how to use a tally system of recording, making a vertical stroke for the first four vehicles (////) and a horizontal stroke crossing through these for the fifth vehicle (////). This system makes it easier to count the total figure.

Back in the classroom the children should display their information by drawing graphs, or using a data processing computer program. You will then need to discuss, as a class, how this data contributes to their investigation, and what other data they may now need to collect. Do they need to repeat the survey at a different time, or at a different location? Would it be helpful to interview pedestrians, or drivers who use the road regularly? Finally they need to decide how to publicise their findings, for example, in the school magazine or the local paper.

Technology for information

This is the one area within the curriculum which has shown rapid development over recent years. It is also an area where some children's knowledge often supersedes that of the adult(s) in the classroom. Many children have access to technological systems that are beyond the financial reach of the primary school. Yet we must be conscious of education for the twenty-first century, where children need to be equipped to deal with a rapidly changing technological society.

Children need to be helped to see the computer as a tool for finding and communicating information which may come in a variety of forms including text, pictures and sounds. They also need to be made aware that the information is gained logically, through a series of steps and using specific commands. It is a case of learning and understanding how the computer can access that specific information as required.

Access to a variety of information is now available through traditional databases, CD-ROMs, and now the Internet; future developments are endless. Technology is becoming more and more exciting where multimedia resources – graphics, sound and video – offer children an extra dimension to text. Although the amount of information available via computers is vast, the quality may vary and children need to become discerning users of the available information.

This section on information technology is designed to help children learn about some of the fundamental concepts of accessing and communicating information using a computer.

Children need to be assissted in adapting to the different systems that are available both at home and at school. It is a case of learning how to access that information and building up the skills which will enable the children to use an exciting resource that could possibly revolutionise the way pupils learn in the classroom.

Using the keyboard

Age range
Five to eleven.

Group size
Pairs.

What you need
Computer, document stand, a timing device, a word processor such as *Pendown* (Longman) or *Creative Writer* (Microsoft), paper for work cards.

What to do
Keyboard skills play a very important role in the effective and efficient use of the computer. The aim of this activity is for children to build up speed and accuracy when using a keyboard in any way. The activity works best if it is carried out in short frequent sessions.

Make three sets of work cards. On the first set write out the letters of the alphabet, at random, in lower case; on the second write out upper case letters at random; on the third write out a variety of letters – upper and lower case. Grouping the letters in sets of two or three will also encourage children to use the space bar efficiently.

Begin with the first set of cards, giving each pair one card. Ask the children to place their card in the document stand which should be positioned next to the keyboard. Set up the word processing software so that children can type on to a blank page. You may want to adjust the size of the font depending on the age of the children.

Tell the children that you want them to try to memorise where the letter keys appear on the keyboard. Ask them to type out all the letters on the work card, but stress that you want them to try to do this without looking at the keyboard and as quickly as possible. The children should work together in their pairs, taking turns to type and to time each other. They can also print out the letters once they have completed their work card to check how accurate they were.

Having carried out a number of sessions using the first card, introduce the second work card. This card involves the children in using the Caps Lock key. They should repeat the same process as before.

Finally, introduce the third card. This card is more difficult than the previous two as it involves the use of the Shift key and, initially, is likely to slow the typing down.

Encourage the children to use both hands for the typing, using all of their fingers rather than just one or two. Show them how to keep their hands in position over the keyboard instead of curling unused fingers into a fist shape. Also introduce the idea of using the thumbs for the space bar.

As the children become more familiar with the layout of the keyboard, challenge them to achieve faster times – beating their own previous times and their partner's times, but without sacrificing accuracy!

Follow-up

Write some simple sentences on other cards, using well-known sayings such as 'More haste, less speed'. This will encourage children to learn the position and use of the punctuation keys.

Mouse skills

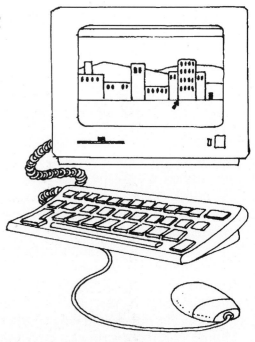

Age range
Five to eleven.

Group size
Pairs.

What you need
A computer, a mouse, software such as *My world* (SEMERC) and appropriate files (see 'What to do').

What to do
Load the software or show the children how to do this. For younger children activities like *Dressing Teddy* or *Nursery* are ideal, or for older children *Design a Castle* or *Town and Village* are suitable (all produced by SEMERC). In these activities children will learn how to select pictures and drag them to new positions on the screen by holding down the select button and moving the mouse pointer to where the picture is to be positioned. For some activities quite fine motor control is needed to position accurately part of teddy or a building in the village.

Use of games such as *Solitaire* (Microsoft) will also encourage the development of similar skills.

More mouse skills

Age range
Five to eleven, depending on experience.

Group size
Pairs.

What you need
A computer with a mouse, a simple graphics program, such as *Ist Paint* (Keyboard Technology Ltd), *Kid Pix 2* (TAG Developments).

What to do
Load the program, or teach the children how to load the program, or let them load the program themselves! Make sure the mouse is in position.

Let the children select a colour by positioning the mouse pointer on the colour of their choice and clicking the select button on the mouse. This is usually the left mouse button although you may be able to reprogram the mouse for left-handed users. Then select a drawing tool, which might be a pencil or a spray can. You may also want to select the thickness of the pencil line or the density of the spray can.

Once the selection has been made, move the mouse to the drawing area of the screen and click the select button. Moving the mouse across the screen immediately with the select button held down allows the child to begin drawing. Releasing the select button on the mouse makes a break in the line. Let the children experiment with colours and lines to begin with, then encourage them to create particular drawings which may be linked with your theme or topic.

Follow-up
Encourage the children to develop their drawing skills and allow them to print out their drawings. They could be introduced to other features such as rollers and brushes to create different effects, or drawing specific shapes, resizing them and filling them with colour.

Write a story – using a word processor

Age range
Six to eleven.

Group size
Two children per computer.

What you need
A computer with a word processor, such as *Pendown* (Longman) or *Creative Writer* (Microsoft).

What to do
The aim of this activity is to use the computer or word processor as a tool in the writing process. It supports children's scanning skills and encourages rapid reading, as children skim (or 'scroll') through their work on the screen in order to improve it.

Ask the children to plan a story, using photocopiable page 124 for support, if required. Model some of the children's plans on the board, and help the children confer with each other on their ideas. Make sure that the children feel confident enough to share their ideas and thoughts.

Depending upon the number of computers available, let the children key in the plan, making sure that the headings give a clear indication of the content that will follow. The important thing about using a word processor is that in the initial stages the writer can explore creative ideas without worrying too much about form, layout or mistakes!

Make sure that the children are building up their keyboard skills because otherwise this can slow down the creative flow. Younger children may need help at first with their typing until their speed increases. Show the children how

to save their work with a relevant and understandable file name and then remind them to save their writing regularly to avoid losing all their hard work.

If a child is experiencing difficulties with the creative ideas, or developing his plan, save the document and print out what has been written so far, close down the file, and let him work with a friend to develop on what he has already achieved.

Once the draft has been completed, encourage the children, in their pairs, to discuss the content and then the layout and spelling. In reality they will be developing their own editing group! Help the children to understand how to 'cut and paste' sentences and paragraphs in order to restructure the piece of writing if necessary. Help them to find the spellcheck to run through the spelling. However, you will need to point out that the alternative spellings that the spellcheck produces are not always appropriate and that they may need to click on 'Ignore'! Each time they read their writing, the children will be engaging in rapid reading and skimming skills, and also working at ways of self-improvement in the writing process.

Once finished, let each child print out her story and either compile them in a book or display them on the wall.

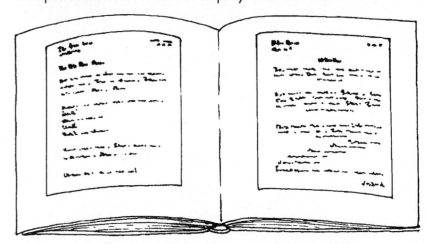

Follow-up

Devise other opportunities for children to use the word processor as a tool for support in writing. For example, let the older children write stories for the younger classes, letting them design their own book cover too.

Information gathering

Age range

Seven to eleven.

Group size

Individuals or pairs.

What you need

A computer with a CD-ROM drive, various information packages such as *Microsoft Encarta* (Microsoft), *The Hutchinson Multimedia Encyclopedia* (Helicon) or *Children's Micropedia* (ESM).

What to do

Before going to the computer, the children need to plan carefully the information they want to find. They need to ask themselves questions such as 'What do I want to find out? What is the best way of doing this? How can I focus on achieving the information I want?'

There is so much information available through CD-ROMs that it is important that children learn to focus on the information they want, because otherwise they can easily become side-tracked into other areas. It is also important that children are aware how different types of CD-ROMs work. For some you may need a direct search using keywords; for others it may be possible to 'browse' through interlinked articles.

Take, for example, a child wanting information on Magellen because the class are learning about explorers. She also wants information about Portugal. She needs to search through the index to decide which category she should use to find further information. She could skim through 'countries' or 'famous people' or even 'continents'. However, she needs to decide how to access the most relevant information. The skills used for finding information in books are also relevant here, the difference being that the information is more interactive between the user and the computer.

Another child may search for Magellen to start with, but once he arrives at this article other interesting links are highlighted. By clicking on the highlighted word the child is automatically taken to another reference which may, or may not, be relevant. It is easy to get lost in such an environment and children need to place bookmarks in relevant pages so they can easily return to them later on.

Information for younger children relies heavily on moving images and comic strips. What is exciting is that very young children can absorb a large amount of information, because they are not so reliant on written text for assimilating knowledge.

Follow-up

Give the children opportunities to evaluate the effectiveness of their planning. How well did they actually achieve what they set out to do? Let them work in their pairs to compare notes. This gives them opportunities to learn from each other and learn from each other's mistakes. The more the children use the system, the more familiar they will become, and thus their competence should increase.

As schools begin to gain access to the Internet children will want to search for information using the 'World Wide Web'. This is similar to accessing a CD-ROM, except that instead of taking you to another section of the CD-ROM the Internet will take children to information stored on a computer, possibly on the other side of the world. The need for careful planning is even more important at this level.

What information do I need?

Age range
Nine to eleven.

Group size
Whole class, then small groups.

What you need
Access to a CD-ROM encyclopaedia and word processing package such as *Pendown* (Longman) or *Creative Writer* (Microsoft).

What to do
Many children are now using CD-ROMs at home and school to research information. Children will often print out the complete text from the CD-ROM entry without picking out the important or relevant information. This

activity will encourage children to look more closely at information needed and to précis what they have found.

Discuss with the class the importance of selecting relevant information from a CD-ROM. A printout from a particular search could be used to introduce the activity. Don't start with too much text – half a page will be enough. You will also need to save the information on to a disk as a plain or ASCII text file (text which has no formatting or text effects such as bold or italics). It is important that children learn how to do this using the school's computers and understand that different CD-ROMs may achieve this in different ways. This plain text can then be loaded into a word processor and reworked by the children (working in small groups) to produce a final version of their information.

Each group will also need a printed copy of their text to work on away from the computer. Discuss with the children how to pick out the key points by looking for keywords and phrases from the text. This will give them further practice at skimming and scanning skills and reading for the main point. The children could use a highlighter pen to identify the important sections. Once this has been done, they can return to the computer to edit the original text.

To do this, the children will need to be shown how to move around the screen using the mouse, remove unwanted text by highlighting and deleting it using appropriate commands, move sections of text around using 'cut and paste' or 'drag and drop' commands and close up any gaps created by the removed sections of text.

Once this has been achieved, the children will need to edit the text to ensure that it flows properly and that things are in the right order. They may need to add linking passages, check punctuation, reorder sections or add their own ideas and information. When this has been done, they can decide how to present their work, changing the font styles and the formats for the layout of the text. These activities will give children opportunities to develop some of the higher order language and word-processing skills.

The final versions should be printed out and displayed next to the original text. Different groups could compare the final versions to see if they have come to the same conclusions about the key points.

Follow-up

Once children have become competent at the editing process they could use the same techniques to work on longer examples for their own topics. They could also be given a maximum number of words to work to and shown how to use the word count facility of their word processor to check their progress.

Floor patterns

Age range
Five to eleven.

Group size
Small groups of four or five.

What you need
A computer with a 'Turtle Graphics' program, and a 'Floor Turtle' or a programmable floor robot such as 'Roamer' or 'PIP', large sheets of sugar paper, a ballpoint pen, coloured felt-tipped pens.

What to do
This activity helps children to develop logical thinking. It also helps them to realise that the computer is a tool that responds to commands that are given step by step. In a sense it gives young children early experience of 'programming'.

Make some cards which show simple directional patterns, including arrows to indicate directionality. Ask the children to type in commands for the Turtle so that it can move in

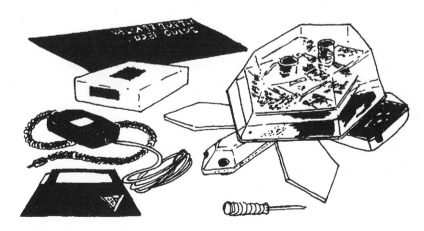

the same direction as the patterns on the cards. For this they need to use either the four arrows on the computer keyboard, or the appropriate commands such as Forward (F), Backward (B), Left (L), Right (R). (These may vary according to the software being used.) The children need to work out how far the Turtle will move with each command. For example, L4; F6; R2; R2; R2; B1. Place a pen in the Turtle so that it can draw the pattern on the paper as it moves so that the children can see how well they have copied the desired pattern.

Alternatively, the children can program the Roamer by pressing the appropriate commands on the touch sensitive keypad on the Roamer itself and watching the pattern it achieves.

Follow-up
Put different coloured pens into the Roamer or Turtle and let the children attempt to design a floor pattern for their friends. Can the friends work out the design by commanding the Turtle to move at the right pace in the correct direction? This can be developed further by making the patterns more complicated.

Using databases

Age range
Five to eleven.

Group size
Two children per computer.

What you need
A computer loaded with a database program, such as *Junior Pinpoint* (Longman).

What to do
This activity is best undertaken within the context of other work being done by the class. Suitable topics might include a database about the children's physical characteristics, the weather, kings and queens from a specific period of history, the buildings along the local shopping street, a traffic survey or a survey of houses in an estate agent's. In this example, the school dinner menu has been selected to link with a project on healthy eating.

Explain to the children that a database program is an ideal way of storing data that you want to collate and analyse later. Tell the children that you are going to set up a database. The children may want to find out how often chips are on the menu because as a class they are looking at diets and what constitutes a healthy diet.

The starting point should then be 'What information do we want from our database?' It is important that the children have some idea of the sorts of questions that they may want to ask once the database is completed. This could be done as a group or class discussion.

Having done this, the children then need to decide on the field names for the database. These are the headings under which data is to be collected. Each separate record on the database will contain a number of different field names. The headings can be any item that you wish to store data on.

You will also need to decide what field type each field will be. There are a number of different field types which can make entering of data easier and the final database simpler to use:
• numeric field (numbers only, ideal for calculations and graphs);
• alphanumeric (numbers, letters and punctuation);
• logical field (true or false, yes or no);
• date (allows dates to be entered easily).
Based on these decisions, the fields can then be created

in the database. For this example:
- date (date entry type);
- chips on menu (true or false);
- number of children eating chips (numeric);
- vegetables available (alphanumeric).

date	chips on menu	number eating chips	vegetable
1.3.1995	y	62	sweetcorn
2.3.1995	n	0	carrots
3.3.1995	y	73	peas
6.3.1995	n	0	tomatoes
7.3.1995	n	0	green beans
8.3.1995	n	0	sweetcorn

Working in pairs, let the children take turns to type in or 'enter' the dinner menus. They can do this in two ways: by finding a list of menus for the past six weeks from the cook; by collecting the information as it occurs daily.

At another time, you may decide to record main courses and desserts in order to use the database to analyse the dessert menu for sugar content. If so, create a new database in the same way and enter in the new field names required.

The children need to decide how they want to retrieve the information. This may involve sorting the records in a different way, perhaps the numbers eating chips from highest days to lowest days. Any numeric fields can also be used to calculate totals, for example the average number of children eating chips. Children could set up searches to find which vegetables are the most popular, or if there is a connection between the days chips are served and the vegetables available.

Most databases also have graphical facilities so that children could draw graphs using the data, for example a bar chart of the dates chips were available and the numbers eating them, or a pie chart showing the distribution of the various types of vegetables on the daily menu.

Follow-up

Databases can also be used for storing data from many areas of the curriculum. It is important that enough time is available for children to build the database and to use it. The use of databases encourages children to think in a logical way. Add more complex searches such as: On which days did the menu include chips *and* sweetcorn? On which days were there chips *or* sweetcorn?

The children need to learn that a computer is a tool for information retrieval. The more organised and logical the children are in the collection, systematic arranging and entering of their data, the more useful will be the information that they can retrieve from their database.

School bookshop

Age range
Nine to eleven.

Group size
Small groups.

What you need
A range of books to sell at school (negotiate this with your local bookshop as they will often let you keep ten per cent of all sales), a computer with a database program such as *Junior Pinpoint* (Longman), notebooks, pencils.

What to do

When you and/or the children have selected the books that you want to sell, you will need to:
- keep a record of all the books so that you can collect the right amount of money;
- know which books you have in stock;
- recognise popular authors;
- predict which books will need to be reordered.

The best way to organise this is to type the details into a database. You will need to decide the field names, for example title, author, price, number of copies in stock, publisher. You could include other specific information such as the ISBN number or date entered into stock. Ask the children to key in the details for each book. This may seem time-consuming, but the database will enable children to sort books either by alphabetical order of title or author, cost, and enable them to search for specific information about the bookshop and its use.

Once the information is in the program, you will have a complete stocklist; you can program the database to calculate the total value of the books, see how long a book has been in stock, check off each book as it is sold, and reorder as necessary. This is an ongoing task which offers

children real responsibility and challenge. It will also develop their information technology skills, support language skills such as alphabetical order, classification skills and skills of prediction.

Follow-up

You might like to encourage the children to take on a long-term task of categorising either the class or school library. It is an excellent way for children to become more involved and responsible for books. Children could also categorise books on keywords so that other children could search for books about space, or those with information about pets. If children tackle this task they may find it useful to use one of the specialised library software packages which also allows them to record the loan of books using a bar-code reader.

Flow charts

Age range
Seven to eleven.

Group size
Whole class, then pairs.

What you need
Pencils, paper, computer, word processor or 'drawing' program.

What to do
Flow charts help children to think clearly and systematically. They also encourage logical thinking by making the children take apart a process and outline it step by step. This clarity of thinking is important for learning to direct and 'program' any computer.

First of all, ask the children to suggest activities or processes that can be broken down into steps, for example making a bed, grilling some toast, tying shoelaces, making a cup of tea, the digestive cycle, the water cycle and so on. Record this information on the board. Then, as a class, take two or three examples and try to define the process. What are the main steps that need to be recorded? Write down the children's ideas as they offer them. Make sure that the process is clear and that no stages have been left out. Try to make the flow chart as concise as possible. Once the ideas are complete, draw a box around each stage, and then draw arrows to show how one stage leads on from another.

Ask the children to make their own flow charts about a process of their own choice. Children could use a simple word processor to type in each of the steps that they need to make. These do not need to be typed in the correct order as children can use the 'cut and paste' or 'drag and drop' facilities to move the statements around. The final order could be printed out, boxes drawn by hand around each step and the linking arrows drawn in by hand. Some basic formatting commands might be introduced, such as centring to help line up the statements down the middle of the page.

Another approach is for children to use a drawing package in which text can be entered. Each step in the process can be typed in and a box or frame drawn around it. At the start, there is no need to position these in a particular place as they can be moved anywhere on the screen later on. Once each step has been entered, they can be placed on the screen using the mouse to select and drag the box to its new position. Once in place, linking arrows can be drawn using the line facilities of the software. Children can experiment with different shaped boxes for parts of their flow chart, use colour to highlight different parts and change the thickness of the lines or boxes. Once completed, the flow chart can be given a title and printed out and displayed.

Follow-up
Suggest that each child designs a flow chart for their topic work for the next term or half-term. These can be placed in their topic books.

Making a multimedia presentation

Age range
Seven to eleven.

Group size
Small groups – up to six pupils working together.

What you need
A computer, multimedia presentation software such as *Genesis* (Oak Solutions), *Magpie* (Longman), *Hyperstudio* (TAG Developments).

What to do

An important part of children's study skills is to be able to present the results of their research in an interesting and imaginative way. With the advent of multimedia it is important that children develop the skills to make their own multimedia presentations.

Children could present the outcomes of history, geography or science work. The same approach could be used to write an interactive quiz on a certain aspect of their work. This example uses ideas from work on the Romans.

Split the class up into several groups of about six pupils and give each group a different aspect of the Romans to present information about. These could be topics such as houses, soldiers, roads, dress and so on.

Multimedia software allows children to present their information on several different interlinked screens. By 'clicking' on certain parts of one screen the child is taken to another linked screen. You may need to set up an initial structure which has a title page depicting each of the areas to be presented; this could be done with pictures or words.

Each group must then design their presentation using no more than four different interlinked screens. The first might be a picture of a Roman villa with key features labelled. By clicking on the baths another screen would appear giving a more detailed picture and factual information about Roman baths. Arrows would take the children back to the previous page or the main index. Children need to decide what information they are going to include, how to present it in the most interesting way, what pictures to use and how they are going to create them.

Text can be written using a word processor, taken from a CD-ROM and edited, or typed into the multimedia software itself. Pictures can be taken from clip-art collections, drawn using an art or drawing package or hand drawn and scanned into computer format using a hand-held scanner. Information can be placed inside boxes, colours used to make the page interesting and other graphics added.

Once each group has designed and collected its information it can come to the computer and create its quota of pages.

Follow-up

Once children have mastered the basic techniques, they can extend the range of media used. They could add sounds, or their own spoken commentary using a microphone connected to the computer and appropriate software, or music taken from a CD player, music package or keyboard connected through a MIDI (musical instrument digital interface). It is also possible to include pictures taken with a video camera and sequences of moving images. The possibilities are endless!

Has it rained today? Using spreadsheets in the classroom

Age range

Seven to eleven.

Group size

Pairs for information gathering and two to each computer in the classroom.

What you need

Rain-gauges made by the children (from plastic bottles), measuring jars, pencils, paper, a computer with a spreadsheet program, for example *Grasshopper* (Newman), *ClarisWorks* (TAG Developments), *Advantage* (Longman).

What to do

Spreadsheets support children's information gathering and retrieval by providing a means for calculating numbers in a tabular form. Spreadsheets can be as simple or as complicated as desired. Each cell in the table can have either information or a formula embedded in it. A formula enables calculations to take place so that when a number is changed in one cell, the spreadsheet will recalculate all other totals which use that number.

Let each child make a rain-gauge. These can be made easily by cutting a plastic bottle and inverting the top part. Older children can design their own rain-guage (on paper first) and make plans for the materials they will use. Once the rain-gauges are made, place in a safe position outside to catch the rain.

The children will need to measure the rainfall every day, and to list this information on paper. They can either collect their information and then put it on to a spreadsheet or they can update the program at regular intervals.

For this, you or the children will need to create the spreadsheet. They will also need to think about the information that they need. Here is a simple spreadsheet concerning daily rainfall.

date	amount of rainfall (ml)	total rainfall (ml)	average daily rainfall (ml)
20.10.95	3ml	3ml	3ml
21.10.95	1ml	4ml	2ml
22.10.95	0ml	4ml	1.3ml
23.10.95	4ml	8ml	2ml

As each amount is entered, the spreadsheet will automatically calculate the total rainfall in one column, while giving the average daily rainfall in another column. By continuing to collect the data on rainfall, the children can discover the average weekly and then monthly rainfall. They can then analyse the data to find out how much more it rained on one day then another.

Most spreadsheets also provide the children with the possibility of graphical representations. This may be in the form of a bar chart, a pie chart or a line graph.

Follow-up

Use the same method to discover the weekly temperature inside and outside the classroom. Continue to analyse that data in terms of warmest weeks and months. Which is the warmest month of the year? Create graphical representations to show the information visually.

Bias and evidence

Children need to be aware that factual material inevitably includes bias. There are two main ways in which bias can occur. The first relates to the selection of material. Decisions have to be taken about what data should be collected, what questions should be asked, and what information should be communicated to others. Selection of particular material inevitably means that other material is left out. This applies to all kinds of information – written, oral, numerical and pictorial.

A second source of bias arises in the presentation of factual information. The words used, the way a graph is presented, the tone of voice of a speaker – these devices all work to put over a particular bias, even though the author may be unaware of it. It is often easier to detect bias in materials created some years ago, when the climate of ideas was rather different. This can be seen, for example, in sexism in books.

Activities in this section offer some strategies for helping children to be aware of bias.

Tudor people

Age range
Seven to eleven.

Group size
Whole class or smaller group working in pairs (depending on resources available).

What you need
Information books and textbooks about Tudor times. (It may be helpful to include some books published 20 or 30 years ago, as well as recent publications.)

What to do
Give each pair of children one book. Ask them to survey the illustrations, counting the numbers of men and women depicted. Are the numbers equal (or nearly equal)? Or are there many more men than women? If there is a difference, ask the children what they think has led to this difference.

What are the people doing in the pictures? Which activities are restricted to men, and which to women? Is this a true representation of Tudor times? How can you tell?

As a whole class compare the findings from different books. Do they all give a similar picture of life in Tudor times, or do some include more women, and more women in active roles? Why is there a difference between the books? Does the date of publication make a difference? How could we find out what women actually did in Tudor times?

Follow-up
Repeat this picture survey, looking for images of old people, children, rich people, poor people. Are there any black people?

Comic stereotypes

Age range
Seven to eleven.

Group size
Whole class working individually, then in pairs.

What you need
Small cards, each with a different occupational role written on it (for example, doctor, schoolgirl, mother, teacher), paper, pencils, a comic for each pair of children.

What to do
Give each child one small card and tell her to hide it so that nobody else sees what is written on it. Each child should then draw a picture showing the person written on the card. They should try to make it as recognisable as possible.

Display each picture in turn and ask the children to guess what the word on the card was. Talk about the ways in which the children made their pictures recognisable. Did they give girls long hair and skirts? Did the doctor have a stethoscope, and the teacher a piece of chalk? Is this how these people really look, or is it just a device to make the drawings recognisable?

Introduce the word 'stereotype'. Explain that if we want our drawings to be recognisable we often use stereotypes. However, some stereotypes may be exaggerated and may give a negative view of a particular group of people.

Give out one comic to each pair of children. Ask them to pick out a character that they feel has been stereotyped in an exaggerated or a negative way. They may want to look at the words and the story-line as well as the illustrations. Ask each pair to present their findings to the rest of the class, either in a discussion or as a display.

Follow-up
Examine books in the classroom for stereotyped images. Illustrations in textbooks can be particularly stereotyped, showing scientists with beards and wearing white coats, for example, or secretaries with high heels and miniskirts.

Personal bias

Age range
Seven to eleven.

Group size
Whole class or smaller group.

What you need
Paper, pencils.

What to do
This activity should take place after the class has been playing a team game such as rounders or football. Ask the children to write an account of the game they have just

played. Emphasise that their account should be written from the point of view of their own team.

Compare accounts written by the two teams. How do they differ? 'An excellent goal' for one team may be 'a lucky fluke' for the other. 'A clear foul' from the perspective of one team may become 'bad refereeing' from the other team's point of view. 'Skilful play' for one side may be seen as 'cheating' by the other team.

In a similar vein, children who support opposing football teams could write accounts of a televised match. Alternatively, you could ask children to write reviews of a television programme or film which only some of them enjoyed.

Discuss how accounts of anything show the opinion of the writer, and the fact that all reporting may incorporate bias.

Follow-up

Examine reports in different newspapers of a particular sporting event, or reviews of a specific television programme or film. Identify similarities and differences between the accounts. Draw the children's attention to the way that the use of certain vocabulary can give a particular impression. (A classic example of this is the difference between the terms 'rebel' and 'freedom fighter'.)

Witness!

Age range

Seven to eleven (can be adapted for younger children).

Group size

Whole class working individually.

What you need

A co-operative friend who is willing to visit the school and act a specific role, paper, pencils. (A cassette recorder may be required for younger children.)

What to do

You will need to arrange for your friend to come into school and stage some sort of incident. For example, he or she could enter the classroom at a time when all the children are sitting together on the carpet, and act the role of a health and safety inspector demanding to see various aspects of the classroom. Another role might be that of a very demanding and noisy prospective parent, or an unwelcome intruder (but take care not to frighten the children). Whatever role is taken, it should be one which will capture the children's attention.

After the incident, ask the children to write an account of what happened, putting down as much detail as possible as if they were witnesses in court. They should do this individually and should not compare notes.

When all the accounts are complete, get some of the children to read out what they have written to the class. Are there any differences in their record of the order of events, or the appearance of the visitor? If they wrote down any of the conversation which took place, does everyone agree about what was said? Are some accounts more detailed than others?

Discuss with the children why there are differences in their versions of what happened. Is it possible for the whole class to agree on a single version? Talk about the implications of the differences in their accounts. What would have happened if they had been asked to be witnesses in a court of law?

(Younger children could carry out the same activity as a discussion, without writing their accounts of the incident, but perhaps recording them on tape.)

Follow-up
Collect together a number of accounts of a particular event from different newspapers and compare them.

The British Empire

Age range
Nine to eleven.

Group size
Whole class or smaller group working in pairs.

What you need
A selection of information books about Victorian times.

What to do
Give each pair two books and ask them to look up the British Empire in both books, using the contents page or the index. Tell them to read and discuss all the information given.

Do the two books give similar accounts? How are they different? Whose point of view is expressed in the books? What do they say about the feelings of the people living in lands which became part of the British Empire?

Encourage the children to look at the sort of language used to explain how the British Empire began. Do the authors use words like 'acquire' and 'gain' which do not indicate any conflict? Or do they use words such as 'invade' or 'conquer', which indicate that there was often opposition and some fighting?

In what ways do the books indicate that the British Empire was a good thing? Do they talk about profits made from goods imported from the Empire? Do the authors express any reservations about the Empire? As a whole group, discuss whether historical accounts should include alternative points of view.

Follow-up
Compare the language used in accounts of the British Empire with the language used to describe other territorial gain – for example, the Norman invasion in 1066, or the German invasion of other European countries in the Second World War.

Contemporary images

Age range
Nine to eleven.

Group size
Whole class or smaller group.

What you need

A variety of pictures illustrating a specific historical period. Some of these should be in the form of drawings, paintings or photographs made at that time; others should be modern representations of the historical period. (Many information books for children include a range of appropriate contemporary and modern illustrations.)

What to do

Identify which pictures are modern and which were created at the time. Are there any differences in what is represented?

Discuss with the children which pictures provide the better evidence. They will need to consider the purposes for which each picture was created. For example, a contemporary portrait of an Elizabethan nobleman may exaggerate his good looks and the richness of his costume because the artist wanted to flatter him.

Discuss whether photographs are likely to be more accurate representations than drawings and paintings. Is it true that 'the camera cannot lie'? The children need to understand that photographers select the images they include in their pictures, just as other artists do, and that this selection can lead to a distortion of the truth.

Finally, do modern drawings in history reference books offer any better evidence? How did the artists decide what to draw? What evidence was available to make the drawing accurate?

Follow-up

Invite a photographer from a local newspaper to visit the class and talk to the children about how the subjects of photographs are selected and what sort of things may be deliberately omitted.

See also the next activity 'Photographic bias'.

Photographic bias

Age range

Nine to eleven.

Group size

Whole class, then groups of three or four children.

What you need

A display of photographs of places collected from newspapers, holiday brochures, geography books, travel books, estate agents' details and so on, a camera and film.

What to do

Talk about the display of photographs and discuss whether the pictures offer an accurate record of what each place is like. How did the photographer decide what to include? The children may have seen holiday programmes on television which reveal that hotels portrayed in brochures as very attractive are actually surrounded by rubbish dumps or building sites. Or they may have seen details about houses for sale where the house pictured looks quite different from the actual house!

Ask the whole class to identify different ways in which the school and its immediate surroundings could be portrayed. For example, you could select only modern features or only old features; children could be shown only when they are working hard or only when they are being unruly; you could pick out litter and untidiness or order and neatness.

Tell each group to choose a particular perspective from which to make a photographic record of the school and its immediate surroundings. You will need to let one group work at a time, so that the camera can be shared. When all the groups have completed their work, make a display of the photographs.

Study skills in projects

This section is rather different from the rest of the book. It offers two examples of projects in which many of the aspects of study skills discussed in previous sections are incorporated. 'Toys' is suitable for younger children and provides a number of individual activities that can be developed from a popular infant topic. 'Travel' is designed for older children and provides activities that link together to form a coherent project. Both projects show how children can make use of a wide variety of data in the course of a particular investigation.

Study skills are most effectively developed in a meaningful context. When children are enthusiastic to find out information for a particular purpose, they see more point in developing effective strategies, and they often surprise themselves with their success in using data sources which at first appear daunting.

Toys

Using the theme of 'Toys', young children can explore and develop their learning through firsthand experience. Most children will have a lot of prior knowledge about toys on which to base their subsequent learning, and it is a topic that holds all children's interest. It can also be linked in with work across the curriculum, through looking at the history of toys, for example. Children will gain a greater understanding of historical concepts if they work on something they know about. Their parents or grandparents may have kept toys from their childhood which the children could compare and contrast with their own. The theme can be used to support a wide range of study skills, for the children will constantly be rehearsing indexing skills, enquiry, evaluation and other techniques which are required in all areas of learning.

My teddy bear went to...

Age range
Five to seven.

Group size
Whole class.

What you need
No special requirements.

What to do
This is great fun as a time filler, but at the same time it serves to reinforce alphabet skills. Start the game by saying, 'My teddy bear went to Amsterdam.' Invite the children to continue. For example, they might say, 'My teddy bear went to Bath.' It does not matter where the bear goes; the destinations can be local ones known to the children or they might be countries or places they have heard of. The important feature is that the destinations must all begin with the letters of the alphabet in the correct sequence.

Follow-up

Once the children have had plenty of practice, try playing this as a memory game. Each person repeats the sentence, adding another destination to the list. For example: 'My teddy bear went to Amsterdam, Bath, Cardiff, Doncaster and Ealing.' 'My teddy bear went to Amsterdam, Bath, Cardiff, Doncaster, Ealing and France.' Continue as far as the children can remember!

Which is the oldest?

Age range

Five to seven.

Group size

Whole class.

What you need

A selection of teddy bears of varying age, a long strip of paper for a timeline, pens, felt-tipped pens.

What to do

For some young children, grasping the concept of time can be difficult. However, the use of timelines helps to increase the child's perception of events occurring at different times.

Ask the children to bring in their teddy bears. Talk about the age of the bears and how long the children have owned them. If possible, include some teddy bears that are older than any belonging to the children. Perhaps you have one yourself or maybe some of the children's parents or grandparents could lend you a bear. The children will need to learn about caring for old bears, too!

Together, decide how old each individual bear is. Then choose a selection of bears to place on the timeline in date order. You will need to choose representatives from

different age groups, so that you have, for example, a day-old bear belonging to a new baby and a forty-year-old bear belonging to a member of staff. Write down the dates of origin of the bears on the timeline. When the bears are removed, the written information is left behind.

Follow-up

Make a display of teddy bears, and let the children draw pictures of their own bear. Read stories about bears, such as *Jane Hissey's Old Bear Stories* (Hutchinson, 1994).

How big?

Age range
Five to seven.

Group size
Whole class working in groups of four.

What you need
The children's teddy bears, Unifix cubes or Multilink, squared paper, coloured pencils or felt-tipped pens.

What to do
Let the children measure their bears with units of non-standard measurement, such as hand spans, then let them measure with Unifix cubes. Discuss the heights of the bears. Which is the tallest? Which is the shortest?

Draw an axis on a large piece of squared paper and write each child's name along the bottom. Then ask each child to place the Unifix cubes by her name. Help her to count the cubes and then ask her to colour in the squares to match the number of cubes used. When everyone has done this you will have a bar chart showing the height of all the bears in the class.

Follow-up
Invite the children to ask questions about the data collected. For example, 'Is it true that Caitlin's bear measures ten Unifix cubes?' Let the children start with true or false questions, then encourage them to ask more open-ended questions.

My favourite toy

Age range
Five to seven.

Group size
Whole class working in pairs and individually.

What you need
Portable cassette recorder, audiotapes, pencils, paper to make a timeline.

What to do
Put the children in pairs and ask them to talk about their favourite toys. Can they give a reason why a particular toy is so special?

Working one at a time, ask the children to interview their parents to find out about their favourite toys when they were children. Can the parents remember which toys were special and why? The children might also be able to interview their grandparents, and possibly even great-grandparents, to find out about *their* favourite toys.

Let the children work in pairs to compare and contrast the findings. Help them to list the similarities and the differences in the toys. What conclusions or assumptions can be made? Who had more toys – the children or their grandparents? Were there similarities in girls' toys, for example? The children could record their findings on a grid similar to the one below:

	Favourite toys
ME	
PARENT	
GRANDPARENT	

Follow-up

Make timeline books depicting the children's findings. Put the timeline at the top of each page. Start off with the children's own favourite toys, and let them draw pictures and write about their toys. Use the next double-page spread to look at the favourite toys of their parents. (Don't forget to be flexible with parental situations.) Continue through the generations until all the information has been recorded.

What's it made of?

Age range
Six to seven.

Group size
Whole class, then pairs.

What you need
A collection of children's toys from pre-Victorian times (if possible) until the present day. (There may be a local museum which could help.) A collection of photographs of toys and of children at play through the generations.

What to do
This activity is designed to support children's skills in investigating and classifying.

Display the collection of modern and older toys, and talk about what they are made of. Group the children in pairs and encourage them to compare and contrast the toys. Help them to list the similarities and the differences. Can they identify what materials the toys are made from? Does the material make a difference? For example, do toys made from plastic last longer than metal ones? If so, why? What toys are made from wood?

Look at some of the dolls. What are old dolls made from? Can their joints be moved easily? Look at building or construction toys. How have they changed? Have any of the constructions toys been in use for some time, like Meccano or LEGO?

Follow-up

Look at different types of moving toys and talk about how they work. Ask the children to design a moving toy. What material would they use to make it? If possible, let them try to make the toy.

Travel

The activities in this section can either be used individually or be linked together to form a project about travel which can be carried out over several weeks. The activities are all aimed at children in junior classes. By this age children are able to sustain interest in a topic over longer periods of time and are able to work more independently than younger children.

Each activity focuses on making effective use of a different kind of reference material which might be used by a traveller: maps, climate maps and graphs, pictures, travel brochures, timetables, reference books. As they pursue their research children will gain skills in using the various types of material. 'Travel diary' offers a way of linking the various activities into a coherent project.

Most travellers begin by looking at holiday brochures. How reliable is the information in this sort of material? 'Selling holidays' helps children take a more critical look at material in brochures and enables them to identify the kinds of bias incorporated. The next stage is packing for the trip. What sort of clothes would you take to Australia or Alaska? What will the weather be like? Use the activity 'Climatic data' to help children find out.

The journey will need to be planned. 'Travel timetables' suggests how children can find out about flights and differences in time zones. Every traveller needs some local currency. 'Exchange rate calculator' tries to simplify calculations of exchange rates. (When planning their journey children could also think about the cost of travel and what sort of budget they would need to work to.)

What does the landscape look like? What crops are grown? Are there large cities? How can one travel around the country? 'Travel maps' suggests ways in which children can use information in atlases to answer these questions.

Travel diary

Age range
Seven to eleven.

Group size
Whole class working individually.

What you need
A wide range of information books about different countries, encyclopaedias, travel brochures, atlases, a globe.

What to do
Explain that each child is going to write a travel diary describing an imaginary visit to a country of his own choice. The diary should be a day-by-day account of the trip and should be based on factual information obtained from reference materials. Tell the children that some materials are available in the classroom, but encourage them to collect more from local libraries or travel agents.

First, ask each child to choose a country to find out about. (You may wish to discourage choices which are not well documented, such as Albania, and countries which children have already visited.) It may be helpful to encourage pairs of children to focus on the same country, as complex reference materials are more easily understood in collaboration. Discuss with the children what information they will need to find out. What attractions are there to visit? Are there any famous historic buildings or safari parks? How can these places be visited? Where can the traveller stay?

When the children have gathered their information they should use it to compile a detailed diary describing an imaginary journey to their chosen country. These will take considerable time to compile and the children may need to

do further research as they go along. The completed travel diary is likely to be a substantial document, incorporating a great deal of research.

Follow-up
Each of the remaining activities in this section focuses on using a different type of material which will enable children to make their diaries more detailed and interesting.

Selling holidays

Age range
Seven to eleven.

Group size
Whole class or smaller group working in pairs.

What you need
Highlighter pens, paper, pencils, holiday brochures relating to the countries the children have chosen to investigate.

What to do

Make sure that each pair of children has a brochure about the relevant country. Then ask them, in their pairs, to choose one page of their brochure to focus on.

Ask them first to highlight all the facts included on that page. It may help if you explain that facts are pieces of information which can be checked. They often involve numbers. For example: 'The average July temperature is 28 degrees Celsius'; 'It takes five minutes to walk from the hotel to the sea front.'

Now ask the children to use a different colour to highlight statements which are opinions. For example: 'the finest of the southern resorts'; 'a place of extraordinary beauty'. Let them make a list of all the adjectives which have been used to make the holiday resort sound more attractive. For example: '*lush, subtropical, supremely colourful* vegetation'; '*sparkling, golden* sands'.

As a whole class, discuss the children's findings and identify how brochure writers make holidays sound attractive. Consider what facts are *not* included in the brochures. For example, temperatures may be given, but rainfall figures omitted. Brochures do not describe traffic jams or pollution. What else has been omitted? Why do brochure writers choose to include some facts but not others?

Follow-up

As a whole class, make a holiday brochure for the local area. Each pair could write about a different local feature, making it sound as interesting and attractive as possible.

Climatic data

Age range
Seven to eleven.

Group size
Whole class working in pairs.

What you need
Photocopiable pages 125–127. You will find graphs for a wider selection of places in many atlases.

What to do
Ask each child to find a climate graph for a town in her chosen country, or at least in a similar part of the world. This graph should be compared with a graph for a UK town near the child's home.

Explain that the graphs show average temperatures and rainfall over several years. Usually, the temperature graph shows the average temperature for each month over the course of one year. Discuss how temperature and rainfall

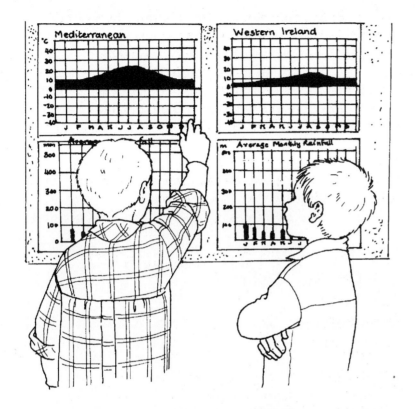

in any particular month can be very different from the average. (Children will probably have heard news reports of months which break all previous records for temperature or rainfall.)

Working in pairs, the children should compare the figures for their chosen travel destination with those for their home area. Is the country they are studying warmer or colder than the UK? Is this the same at all times of year? Is the pattern of seasons similar to that in the UK, or do the highest temperatures occur when it is winter here?

How will this information affect the child's travel plans? Which time of year would be most comfortable for visiting the chosen country? Children may assume that it is best to

go when the weather is hottest on the basis that the holiday season in the UK is when we have the highest temperatures. However, this assumption may be mistaken: very high temperatures are extremely uncomfortable. Other factors will also need to be taken into account. It is best to visit a mountainous area when it is not too rainy, for example. Cloud cover blots out the mountain views.

What sort of clothing would be suitable for the weather? Children should now be able to compile a packing list.

Follow-up
Children could also investigate climate maps in atlases which show temperatures in January and July and annual or seasonal rainfall. Travel brochures and information books about the chosen country may also give information about the weather that can be expected.

Travel timetables

Age range
Seven to eleven.

Group size
Whole class working in pairs.

What you need
Airline timetables (out-of-date timetables are fairly easily obtainable from travel agents), paper, pencils, atlases, maps of time zones (see photocopiable page 128).

What to do
The purpose of this activity is to plan the journey to the chosen country. It will provide practice in extracting information from timetables. Airline timetables can be

Time or British Summer Time for UK departures and arrivals? (Or does this vary with the month the timetable applies to?) Is the time of arrival at the destination shown in GMT or in local time? What is the time difference between the UK and the destination? (Some timetables may state this; alternatively, use the time-zone map on page 128.) How many hours does the flight take? Will it be dark or light when the plane arrives?

Once the children have found all the necessary information, they can plan their journeys and write the relevant sections of their travel diaries.

Exchange rate calculator

Age range
Seven to eleven.

Group size
Whole class or small groups working individually.

What you need
Graph paper, rulers, pencils, list of exchange rates (from newspaper or other source).

What to do
The intention of this activity is to make a ready reckoner which will allow conversion from pounds and pence to foreign currency.

Give each child a piece of graph paper and ask them to draw the axes and then plot pounds along the bottom of the graph. Each child will need to decide what scale to use on the y axis, depending on the exchange rate of the appropriate currency. Check the current exchange rates in a newspaper or at a bank.

quite complex, so it will help if children work together in pairs. When the children successfully extract the information they require they will feel very satisfied!

Help each pair to make a list of major cities in their chosen country which it might be possible to fly to. Large timetables covering more than one country usually have a contents list and/or an index. The children will need to use these to find their intended destinations. They will find that timetables convey a lot of information in a small space. There is generally a key specifying which days of the week any particular flight takes place and what stops are made during the journey.

Once the appropriate section in the timetable has been identified the children will need to find out what time systems are used. Does the timetable use Greenwich Mean

Each child will need to find out how much of the foreign currency is equal to £1 and then select the nearest round number to that figure. This will be the main unit used on the y axis. For example: if £1 = 8.3 French francs, use 10f as the main unit on the y axis; if £1 = 38 Pakistani rupees, use 50 rupees as the main unit on the y axis.

Ask the children to mark a pencil cross on the graph showing the equivalent to £1. Then ask them to calculate the exchange rate for £2 and mark that with a cross. They should join these two points with a straight line using a ruler. The line should also go through (0, 0) and should be extended right across the graph. It will now be possible to convert pounds to the foreign currency by reading the graph. (An example of an exchange rate graph is shown below.)

Exchange rate calculator: Pounds sterling/French francs
£1 = 8.3 francs

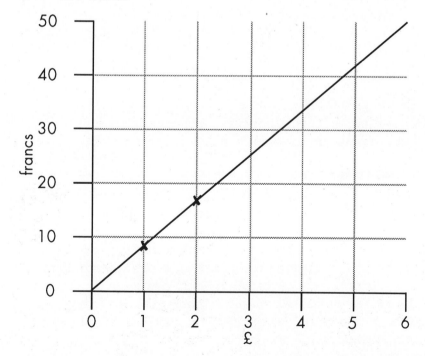

Follow-up

Ask each child to make up three questions which can be answered by using the graph they have made. Then let them swap graphs and questions with a partner and answer each other's questions.

Travel maps

Age range

Seven to eleven.

Group size

Group of eight to ten children. (This activity could be done with the whole class if you have enough atlases to go round.)

What you need

An atlas for each pair of children. A globe or large wall map would also be helpful.

What to do

Choose a country that none of the children have visited. Ask everyone to look at the relevant page of the atlas, or point out the country on a large wall map.

Ask the children what the map tells them about the landscape. Is it mountainous or flat? How high are the mountains? Are there glaciers or ice-fields? Are there many rivers? Where do they flow to? What about cities? How large are they? Are they inland or on the coast? How can one travel around the country? Is there a dense network of roads or railways? The children will need to use the key of the map to make sense of it.

Now ask the children to work in pairs to investigate each of the questions above in relation to the countries they are studying.

Follow-up

The children could compare the map of the country discussed earlier with the map of the UK. How high are the mountains in India, for example, compared with those in Scotland? How do the cities compare in size? (Take care here: the key used for each map tends to be different, so land coloured brown, say, on the map of India will not be the same height as land coloured brown on the map of the UK. One way to get round this is to use a world map or a globe.)

In order to gain more information about their chosen countries, children can use the thematic maps in the atlas. Maps of vegetation and agriculture indicate what the landscape may look like. Many atlases also include maps of population density, and of winter and summer rainfall and temperatures. Some may include information about raw materials and industry.

Reproducible material

The categorising game, see page 14

Name: _____

Categories

Column 1	Column 2	Column 3
Something you eat		
Something made of plastic		
Something made of wood		
An animal		
A vegetable		
An item of clothing		
A fruit		
A flower		
A famous building		
A city		
Something old		
A cartoon character		
Something you'd find at the circus		
A mathematical term		

Setting the questions, see page 16

(Topic) _____

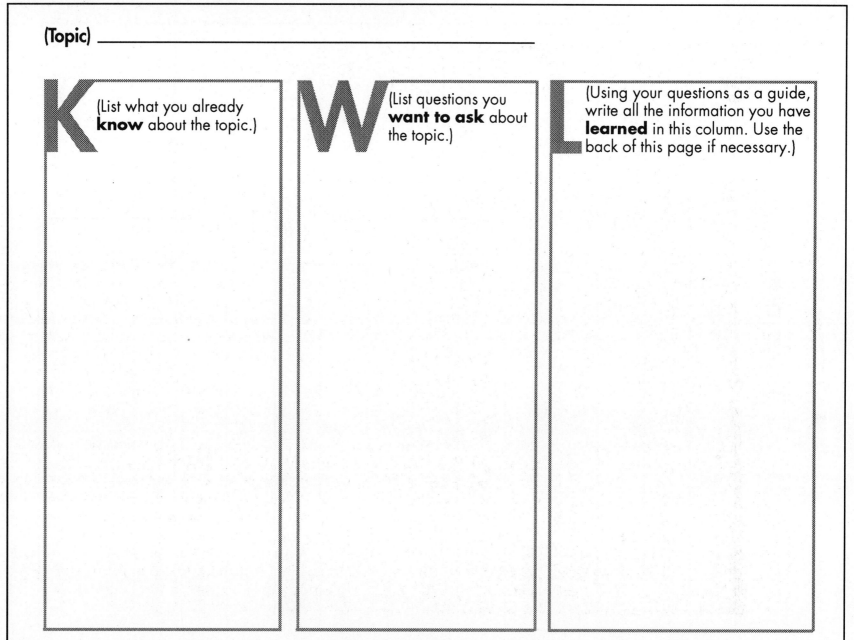

K (List what you already **know** about the topic.)

W (List questions you **want to ask** about the topic.)

L (Using your questions as a guide, write all the information you have **learned** in this column. Use the back of this page if necessary.)

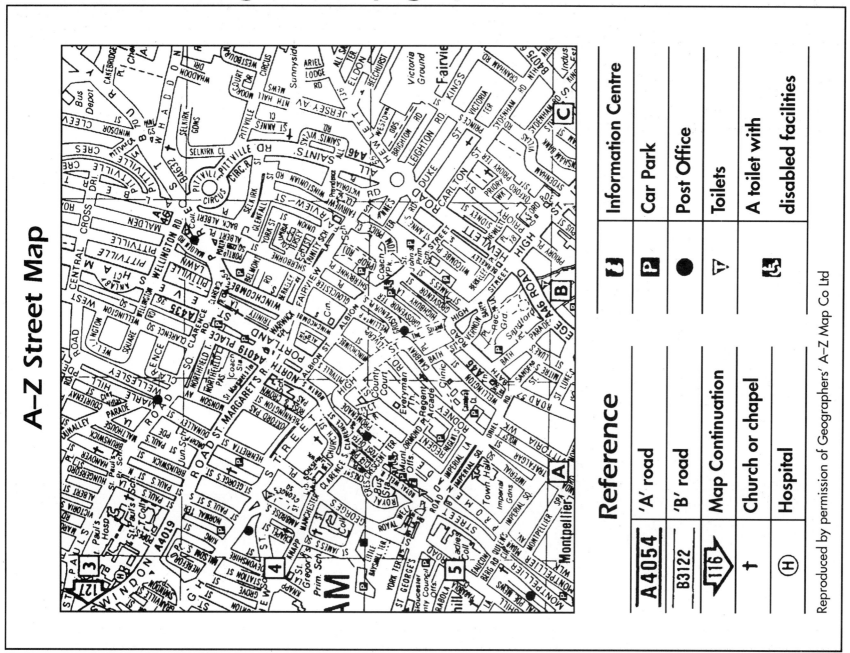

A–Z Street Map

Reference

ℹ	Information Centre
P	Car Park
●	Post Office
▽	Toilets
♿	A toilet with disabled facilities

A4054	'A' road
B3122	'B' road
⬆116	Map Continuation
✝	Church or chapel
Ⓗ	Hospital

Reproduced by permission of Geographers' A–Z Map Co Ltd

Co-ordinates and grids, see page 50

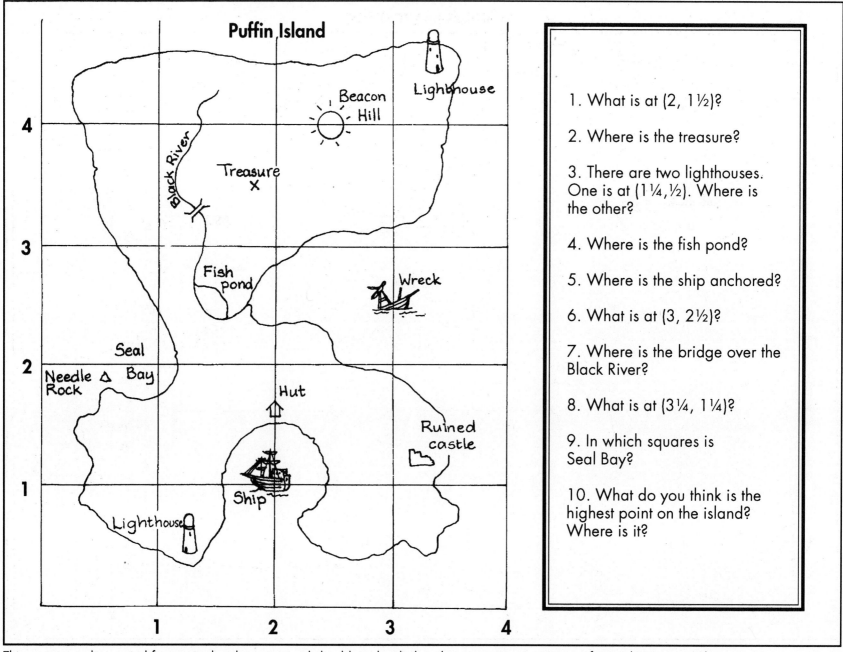

Puffin Island

1. What is at (2, 1½)?

2. Where is the treasure?

3. There are two lighthouses. One is at (1¼, ½). Where is the other?

4. Where is the fish pond?

5. Where is the ship anchored?

6. What is at (3, 2½)?

7. Where is the bridge over the Black River?

8. What is at (3¼, 1¼)?

9. In which squares is Seal Bay?

10. What do you think is the highest point on the island? Where is it?

Great circle routes, and How big is Greenland? see pages 55 and 56

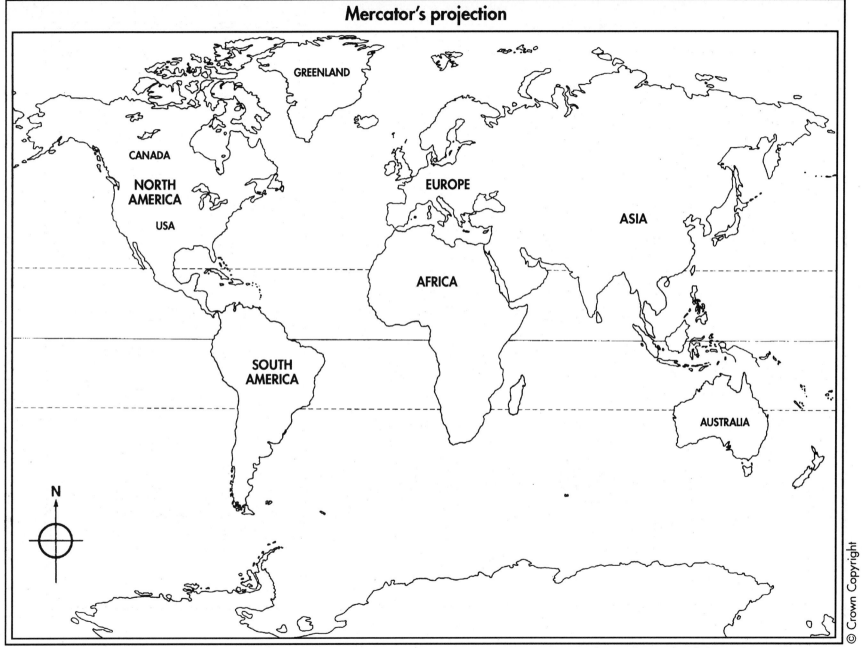

Mercator's projection

GREENLAND

CANADA

NORTH
AMERICA

USA

EUROPE

ASIA

AFRICA

SOUTH
AMERICA

AUSTRALIA

N

How big is Greenland?, see page 56

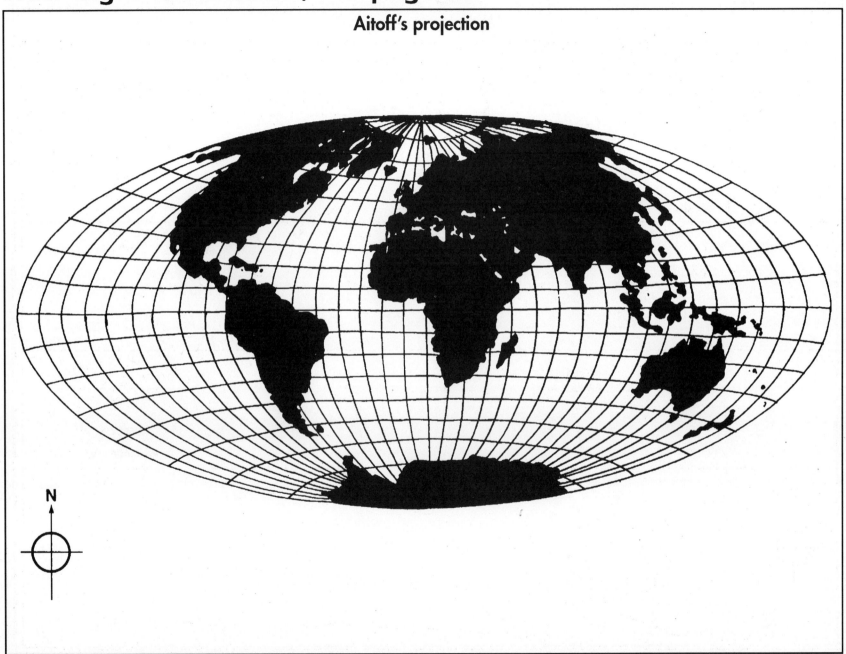

Aitoff's projection

N

How big is Greenland?, see page 56

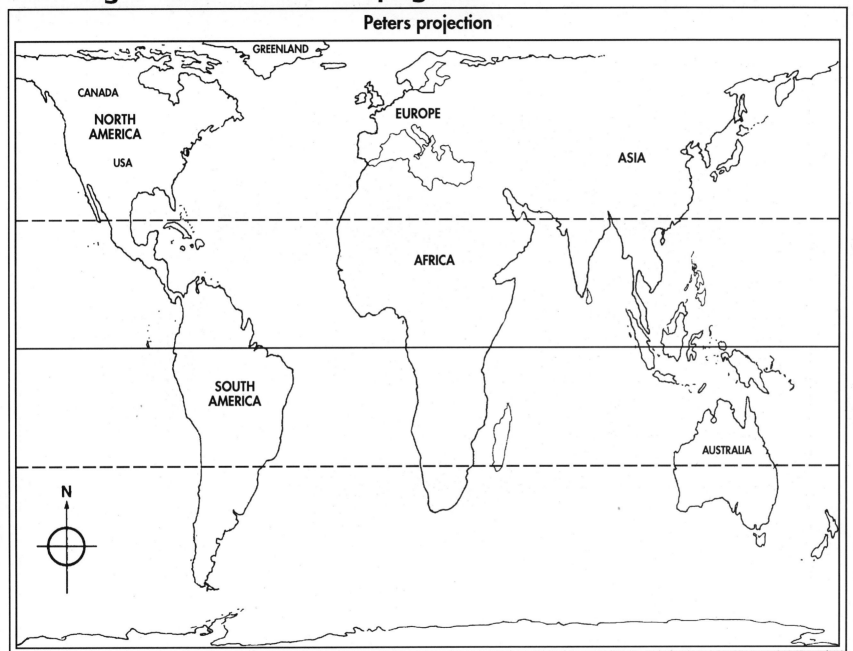

Peters projection

GREENLAND

CANADA

NORTH
AMERICA

USA

EUROPE

ASIA

AFRICA

SOUTH
AMERICA

AUSTRALIA

N

This page may be copied for use in the classroom and should not be declared in any return in respect of any photocopying licence.

1. What is the product being advertised?

2. Who is it aimed at – girls or boys, men or women?

3. How do you know this?

4. What do you notice most – the music, the words spoken, the product, or the people in the advert?

5. List the reasons why you would like to buy the advertised product.

6. List the reasons why you would not like to buy this product.

7. List anything else that you think is important about this advert.

Designing an advert, see page 66

FOR SALE

_____

_____

_____

_____

_____

_____

Headline news, see page 68

Pensioner hits jackpot!

Blizzards bring Wales to a halt

Record run wins gold

Viking treasure trove on Essex farm

Family of four escape blazing flat

Nightmare journey for commuters

Weather reports, see page 71

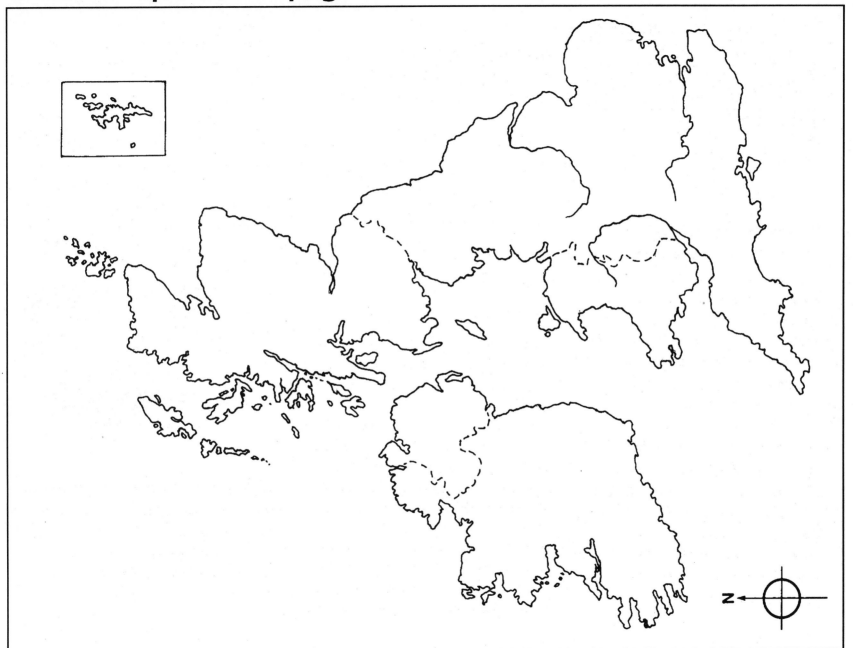

Weather reports, see page 71

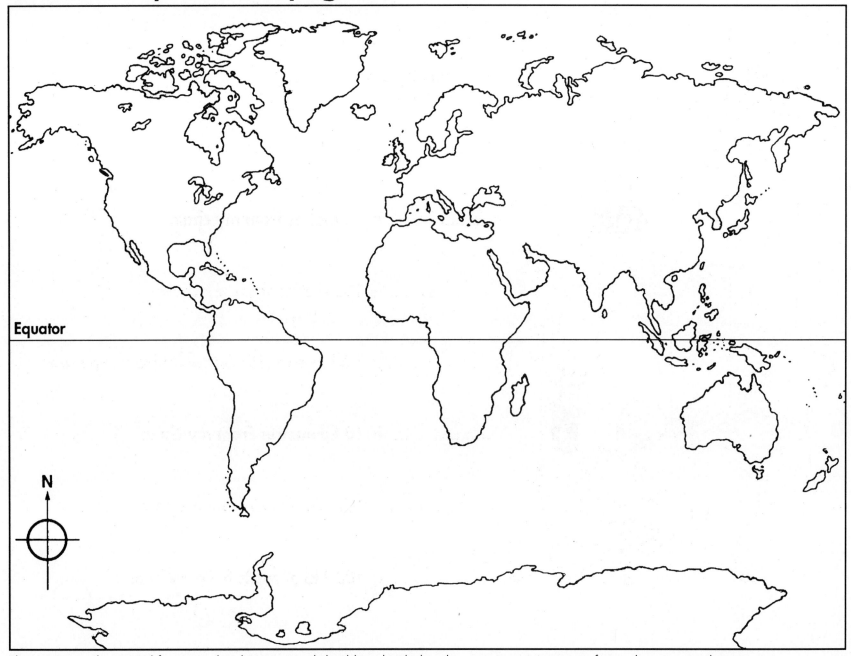

Equator

N

Fill in the blanks.

.... is 1 metre from my chair.

.... is 10 metres from my chair.

.... is 100 metres from my chair.

.... is 1 kilometre (1000 metres) from my chair.

.... is 10 kilometres from my chair.

.... is 100 kilometres from my chair.

.... is 1000 kilometres from my chair.

Write a story – using a word processor, see page 82

Planning sheet

TITLE

CHARACTERS (Who are they? What do they look like?)

SETTING (Where will the story take place? Does the setting change?)

BEGINNING (Think carefully – make it interesting enough
for the reader to want to read on!)

MIDDLE (Extend the story, bring in all the characters. This is
where it all happens!)

END (Bring the story to an end; make sure all the characters
have been involved.)

Climatic data, see page 105

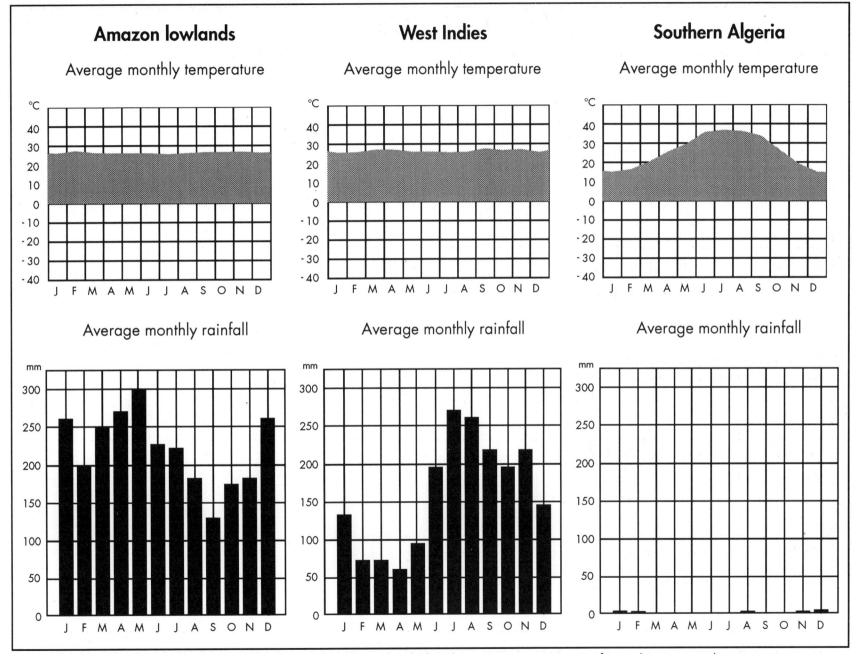

Amazon lowlands

Average monthly temperature

Average monthly rainfall

West Indies

Average monthly temperature

Average monthly rainfall

Southern Algeria

Average monthly temperature

Average monthly rainfall

Climatic data, see page 105

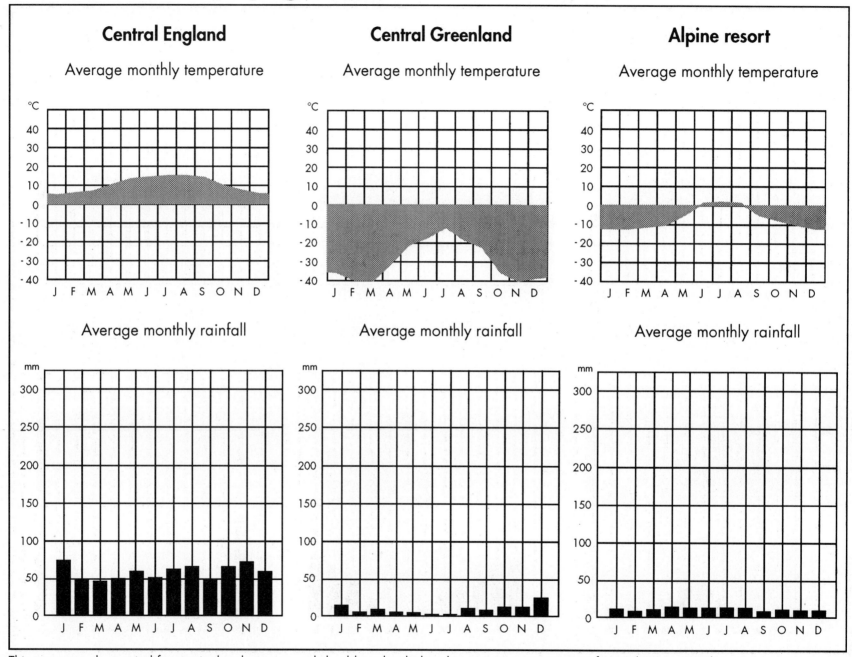

Central England

Average monthly temperature

Average monthly rainfall

Central Greenland

Average monthly temperature

Average monthly rainfall

Alpine resort

Average monthly temperature

Average monthly rainfall

Climatic data, see page 105

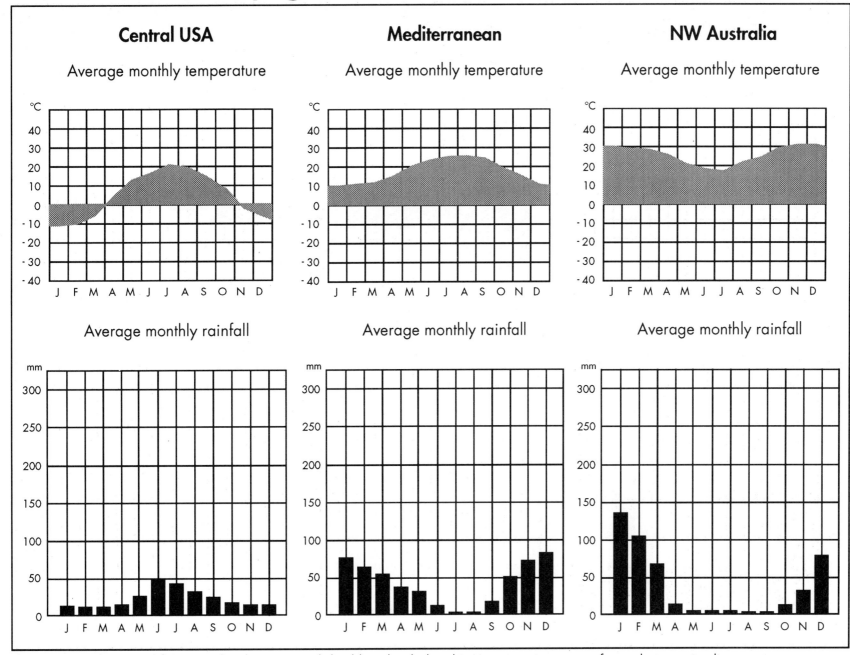

Central USA

Average monthly temperature

Average monthly rainfall

Mediterranean

Average monthly temperature

Average monthly rainfall

NW Australia

Average monthly temperature

Average monthly rainfall

Travel timetables, see page 106

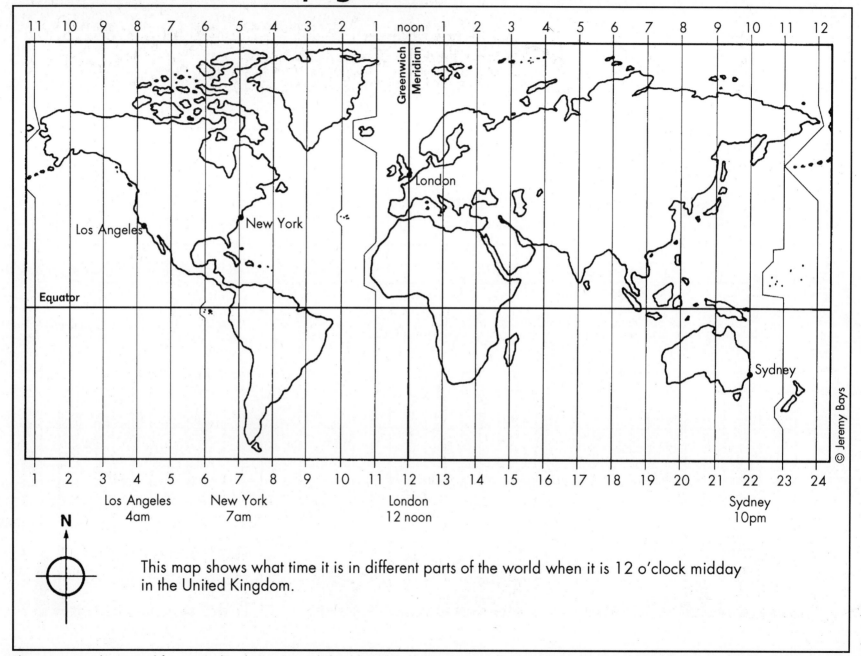

This map shows what time it is in different parts of the world when it is 12 o'clock midday in the United Kingdom.